LAW OF IMMIGRATION AND ENTRY TO THE UNITED STATES OF AMERICA

by Irving J. Sloan

Revised Fourth Edition

Irving J. Sloan
General Editor

1987
Oceana Publications, Inc.
London • Rome • New York

This is the fifth number in a series of LEGAL ALMANACS which bring you the law on various subjects in nontechnical language. These books do not take the place of your attorney's advice, but they can introduce you to your legal rights and responsibilities.

Library of Congress Catalog Card Number: 86-0635-39
ISBN: 0-379-11159-4

TABLE OF CONTENTS

Introduction

HISTORICAL PERSPECTIVE OF IMMIGRATION LEGISLATION

The authority of the United States to regulate immigration issues from its inherent power of sovereignty, and the constitutional authority of Congress to regulate commerce with foreign nations. The power is absolute, vested in the political departments of the government and not subject to challenge. It may be exercised through treaties negotiated by the President with Senate approval, or statutes enacted by Congress. Thus, Congress may specify the terms—arbitrary or otherwise— upon which aliens shall be admitted, or may, in its discretion, exclude them entirely. Furthermore, it may designate the agencies to administer its policies, and so long as such agencies do not transcend their authority or abuse the discretion reposed in them, their judgments are final.

In the early days of the Republic and for almost a century thereafter the government did little or nothing to restrict immigration. On the contrary, early legislation tended to encourage immigration by improving transportation facilities. The first laws having a restrictive effect were designed to preclude the entry of criminals, "immoral" persons, "coolie" labor, and paupers. In 1882 Chinese were barred from acquiring permanent residence in this country, and similar restrictive measures extended this policy until 1943. In 1885 the importation of "cheap" labor was halted by an alien contract labor law designed to alleviate the deleterious effect of such competition on the domestic labor market.

Heavy immigration during the nineteenth century stimulated sentiment for further restrictive measures. Between 1891 and 1910, various classes of undesirables were added to the list of excludable immigrants (including polygamists, persons afflicted with certain mental diseases and disabilities, dangerous or loathesome illnesses, anarchists, saboteurs, persons believing in or advocating the overthrow by force and violence of the United States Governments, all governments, or all forms of law, and still other categories of mental and moral defectives). In spite of these measures, however, the influx of immigrants continued to accelerate.

In response to rising resentment of unrestricted immigration during the First World War, Congress, on February 5, 1917, enacted what then became the basic immigration law, codifying all previously passed restrictive measures, and defining the categories of excludable aliens. Provision was made for inspection of immigrants on arrival, medical examination, and the return of unlawful immigrants. Especially noteworthy innovations were those barring illiterate aliens over 16 years of age and natives of many Asiatic countries.

Until 1921, the basis of excludability was qualitative, rather than numerical—that is, aimed only at immigrants possessing certain undesirable characteristics. In that year, however, with Europeans clamoring to leave that war-ravaged continent, and Americans faced with problems of unemployment and housing, the first quota law came into being, limiting the number of admissible nationals from any one country to three percent of the foreign-born population of that nationality which had resided here in 1910—aggregating a total of 350,000 persons.

After further study and analysis of the new law's effect, Congress, on May 2, 1924, introduced what has since been known as the "national origins quota system." The enactment of that date inaugurated a system of numerical restriction based on the "national origins" of those comprising the population of this country in 1920, instead of the number of foreign-born residents here at any time. The asserted purpose was to arrest the trend toward a change in the fundamental composition of the American stock.

From time to time Congress modified the drastic restrictions of this law by a series of special enactments, such as those facilitating the admission of "war brides" and "GI fiancees" between 1945 and 1948, and easing the entry of "displaced persons" and refugees thereafter.

The present Immigration and Nationality Act (known as the McCarran-Walter Act) was enacted on June 27, 1952. This constituted a revision and codification of the various acts and treaties, implemented by executive orders, presidential proclamations, and administrative regulations which preceded it. It involved no radical departure from trends already manifest in earlier Acts. The national origins quota system was continued, with preferences granted, however, to certain immigrants urgently needed here; provisions made for closer screening of aliens—particularly subversives and security risks—and grounds for exclusion and deportation expanded.

A subsequent series of amendments—particularly in 1957 and 1958—tended to liberalize the law, but the most significant revision came on October 3, 1965 with President Johnson's signature of an Act abolishing the national origins quota system; repealing the Asia-Pacific triangle stipulation; creating new ceilings and priorities; revising the preference classes; and implementing the Act by a variety of new provisions. This obviously ushers in a new era in progressive policy. The partially deferred operation of certain aspects of the Amendment, however, requires an exposition of the pertinent provisions of both the old and the new in order to elucidate the intermediate and ultimate status of the law.

The 1965 legislation did not deal with a number of additional changes proposed by many members of Congress.

A 1966 enactment granted adjustment of status benefits to Cuban refugees, and provided a savings clause for applications for adjustment of status filed by Western Hemisphere aliens prior to December 1965.

A 1970 enactment made the following changes relating to nonimmigrants:

(1) The temporary worker group was enlarged by eliminating the requirement that the temporary work to be performed by those in the distinguished merit category (H-1) must not be in a position which is permanent in nature; by eliminating the word "industrial" in the trainees in agriculture, commerce, finance, government, transportation, or the professions; and by extending the temporary worker category to include spouses and children of such immigrants.

(2) A new K nonimmigrant classification was established for fiancees or fiances of American citizens, and the minor children of such aliens who enter for the purpose of marriage, with provisions for adjustment of status if the marriage takes place within three months.

(3) A new L nonimmigrant classification was established for business executives or managers seeking to come temporarily in order to continue their service for their concerns, and the spouses and minor children of such aliens.

(4) The foreign residence requirements for J exchange visitors was modified by making it applicable only to those whose program was financed by the United States or by their own governments, and to those whose skills are clearly needed in their own countries. Moreover, additional grounds for waiver of the foreign residence requirement were prescribed for exchange visitors who would be subject to persecution upon their return, and those whose countries stated that they had no objection to the waiver.

Two significant immigration statutes were enacted in 1976. The major enactment was designed primarily to correct certain inequities relating to *Western Hemisphere immigrants,* but made a number of additional changes, and its provisions included:

(1) Incorporation of the separate Western Hemisphere quota into the basic law.

(2) Extension of the statutory preference system to the Western Hemisphere quota.

(3) Extension of the annual limitation of 20,000 for each country and 600 for each colony or dependent area (increased from 200) to the Western Hemisphere.

(4) Provision for proportional reassignment among the various preference groups of the annual limitation for any country or dependent area which had oversubscribed its annual limitation during the previous fiscal year.

(5) Modification of the statutory preferences, so that third preference immigrants would thereafter require a sponsoring employer and the fifth preference could thereafter be sought only if the petitioning citizen is at least 21 years of age.

(6) Modification of the labor certification requirement so that labor certifications for teachers or aliens with exceptional ability in the sciences or arts could thereafter be denied only if there are equally qualified persons in the United States.

(7) Modification of the provisions for adjustment of status so that this remedy will hereafter be available to Western Hemisphere aliens and to those for whom an immigrant visa is immediately available at the time their applications are filed, and precluding this remedy for TRWOV aliens, and for aliens (other than immediate relatives) who on or after January 1, 1977 continue in or accept unauthorized employment prior to filing an application for adjustment of status.

(8) Specifically directing that adjustments of status for Cuban refugees who were physically present in the United States on or before January 1, 1977 would not thereafter be chargeable to the applicable immigration quotas.

(9) Two savings clauses were prescribed. The first preserved eligibility and priority under the law then in effect for visa petitions filed prior to January 1, 1977. The second preserved eligibility and priority under the law then in effect for Western Hemisphere immigrants who had established such eligibiliy and priority prior to January 1, 1977. Such Western Hemisphere immigrants would retain their original priority date if a visa petition according them preference status was thereafter approved.

The second 1976 statute was part of the comprehensive Health Professions Educational Assistance Act of 1976. On the basis of a legislative finding that there was no longer a shortage of doctors in this country, the statute imposed severe restrictions on the entry of foreign doctors. These included:

(1) Precluding the entry of foreign medical graduates coming as third, sixth, or nonpreference immigrants principally to perform services as members of the medical profession unless they have passed Parts I and II of the National Board of Examination (or an equivalent examination determined by HEW).

(2) Imposing various restrictions on the entry of foreign medical doctors seeking to come as H (temporary worker) nonimmigrants.

(3) Imposing various restrictions on the entry of foreign doctors seeking to come as J (exchange visitor) nonimmigrants.

(4) Directing HEW to develop adequate data within 1 year to enable the Secretary of Labor to make equitable determinations regarding labor certification applications on behalf of foreign medical graduates.

A number of new statutes were enacted in 1978. One of these abolished separate Eastern and Western Hemisphere quotas, combining them in a single worldwide annual quota of 290,000, and established a Select Commission on Immigration and Refugee Policy to study existing laws. Another provision authorized retroactive adjustment of status for refugees paroled into the United States before September 30, 1980.

A second 1978 statute made a number of changes in the statutory provisions for the immigration and naturalization of adopted children.

The Act of October 10, 1978 repealed and modified various statutory provisions dealing with expatriation to reflect Supreme Court decisions and changed attitudes produced by those decisions.

The Act of October 30, 1978 was directed against persons who participated in persecutions between 1933 and 1945 under the direction of, or in association with, the Nazi government of Germany. Such persons are barred from the United States, subjected to expulsion, and precluded from various benefits under the immigration laws.

The Act of November 2, 1978 liberalized the literacy requirements for naturalization applicants who are over the age of 50 and have lived in the United States for at least 20 years.

The agencies charged with administration of the immigration laws are the Immigration and Naturalization Service headed by a Commissioner under the over-all direction of the Attorney General and the Bureau of Security and Consular Affairs, and is directed by an Administrator under the general supervision of the Secretary of State. The Service regulates the admission of aliens at ports of entry, while the Bureau administers the issuance of visas through its consular officers abroad. These agencies, of course, perform other functions as well, but these are not directly pertinent to the subject of this publication.

The inspection of arriving aliens, apart from their physical and mental examination, is made by one or more immigration officers who are authorized by law to board and search any vessel, aircraft, railway car, or other vehicle for this purpose. Until this process is completed, no passenger or crewman may leave the conveyance which brought him, nor will he be permitted to land. The examining officer may require any person seeking entry to state under oath the purposes for which he has come; how long he intends to stay; whether he intends to remain permanently; and if an alien, whether he intends to become a citizen. The officer may also ask any other questions designed to help him determine the traveler's nationality, and if he is an alien, whether he is excludable. The medical examination is conducted by an officer of the United States Public Health Service (or a contract-location or panel physician).

Every alien (other than a crewman, who may be ordered to be detained on board until his craft departs) who does not appear to the examining officer to be clearly, and beyond a doubt entitled to land, must be detained by a "special inquiry officer" (except that the case of a person suspected of being a subversive or security risk is referred directly to higher immigration authorities). These officials may refuse admission without disclosing the reasons where such disclosure would be prejudicial to the public interest.

An alien detained for further inquiry is notified of such action immediately and in writing by the examining officer. Until afforded a hearing, he is deemed temporarily excluded and may be confined to an immigration detention station unless paroled or released on bond. At the formal hearing before the special inquiry officer, he may be accompanied by a lawyer, friend, or relative, and may offer evidence on his own behalf. In the event of an adverse decision, he may appeal from the order of exclusion to the Board of Immigration Appeals, a panel of officers directly representing the Attorney General. If unsuccessful, the alien must be deported to the country from whence he came, in accomodation of the same class in which he arrived, on the vessel or aircraft bringing him. The expense of retransport must be borne by the owner of such craft. Every safeguard is provided throughout the hearing to protect the rights of the applicant, and immigration personnel are generally known to be considerate and courteous in their approach.

Chapter 1, which follows this historical perspective, brings our discussion up to date with a summary narrative of the most current addition and amendment to the immigration laws of the United States.

The reader is reminded that the foregoing Introduction, as well as the text to follow, is essentially restricted to the subject of the admissibility of aliens.

Chapter 1

THE 1986 IMMIGRATION ACT

In October 1986, Congress passed a landmark immigration law which made the biggest changes in immigration law in at least 20 years. While a study such as this cannot anticipate how the provisions in the law will be interpreted and implemented, the best it can offer the reader is a clear description of the major provisions here at the outset of our work on the law of immigration. The changes which the present legislation make on the immigration law presently existing is incorporated in the subsequent chapters of this Almanac.

The new law contains "sweeping" changes in the way the United States treats *aliens.* Among its important features are a new system of penalties against employers who knowingly hire illegal aliens, amnesty for illegals who came to the United States *before 1982,* and $4 billion in appropriations to help states pay the costs of legalizing foreigners. It also creates a special program to ensure that growers have enough workers to harvest their crops. What follows is a summary description of the major provisions of the new law.

EMPLOYER SANCTIONS

It is unlawful for any person knowingly to hire, recruit or refer for a fee any alien not authorized to work in the United States.

Employers are required to verify all newly hired people by examining either a U.S. passport, a certificate of U.S. citizenship, a certificate of naturalization or a resident alien card. If any of these documents are not available, verification could be established by a combination of papers showing authority to work and identity. For example, a person could show a driver's license in addition to either a U.S. birth certificate or a Social Security card.

Requires each employer to attest in writing under penalty of perjury that he saw such documentation before any hiring.

Requires the employee to attest in writing before being hired that he is authorized to work in the United States.

Permits the President to implement a more secure verification system upon notice and approval of Congress. The appropriate agencies are directed to study the feasibility of a system, like the one currently used to check credit cards, where employers could telephone a central number to get documents verified.

Establishes civil and criminal penalties for hiring illegal aliens but provides a six-month education period during which employers would not be subject to penalties. During the subsequent 12-month period, a violator would be given a warning citation for the first offense.

Establishes the following fines for violation after the citation period:

> *First offense* - a civil fine of not less than $250 nor more than $2,000 per illegal alien found to be hired.
> *Second offense* - a civil fine of not less than $2,000 nor more than $5,000 per illegal alien.
> *Third offense* - a civil fine of not less than $3,000 nor more than $10,000 per illegal alien.

Authorizes criminal penalties of up to six months' imprisonment and/or a $3,000 fine for a "pattern or practice" of knowingly hiring an illegal alien.

Requires employers, recruiters, and those who refer for employment to keep records. The law establishes a civil fine of not less than $100 nor more than $1,000 for failure to keep records.

Allows employers charged with violating the law to defend themselves by showing that they had complied in good faith with the verification procedure.

Requires the Attorney-General to notify alleged violators of the infractions and, upon request, grant a hearing within 30 days before imposing any penalty.

Requires administrative law judges to conduct hearings "at the nearest practicable place" to where alleged violators live and the infractions occurred.

Requires the judge to use a "preponderance of the evidence" as the standard for finding that a violation had occurred.

Makes the decision of the judge final unless the Attorney-General modifies or vacates the order within 30 days.

Gives a violator 45 days from the time the order becomes final to challenge his penalty in a federal appeals court.

Relieves employers from verifying a worker's credentials when a state employment agency had done so and the worker retained a certification of such verification.

Terminates sanctions after three years if the Comptroller General determines that sanctions resulted in discrimination in employment or had unduly burdened employers, and Congress enacts a joint resolution adopting that determination.

Provides expedited procedures for Congress to consider a joint resolution terminating sanctions.

ANTI-DISCRIMINATION MEASURES

Creates an Office of Social Counsel in the Justice Department to investigate and prosecute any charges of discrimination stemming from unlawful immigration-related employment practices.

Bars employers from discriminating against legal residents simply because they were not full-fledged citizens. (However, this provision covers only those permanent or temporary residents who had shown an intention to become citizens.)

Makes clear that an employer could not be sued if, between two equally qualified people, he chose the U.S. citizen over the legal resident who was not yet a citizen. Exempts employers of three or fewer workers from coverage.

Authorizes an administrative law judge, after a hearing, to order a violator to hire the aggrieved person, to award limited back pay if appropriate and to pay a penalty of $1,000 for each individual discriminated against.

Terminates the anti-discrimination provisions if the employer sanctions are lifted. The antibias mechanism also could be ended if Congress, by joint resolution, determined that sanctions had not resulted in discrimination or that the process had "created an unreasonable burden on employers."

INCREASED ENFORCEMENT AND SERVICE

Provides a two-year authorization for the Immigration and Naturalization Service (INS) to receive an additional $422 million in fiscal 1987 and $419 million in fiscal 1988. The law also authorizes $12 million in fiscal 1987 and $15 million in fiscal 1988 for the Executive Office of Immigration Review to carry out added duties for the INS imposed by the law.

Increased criminal penalties for smuggling aliens into the United States. A violator can be imprisoned for up to five years per smuggled alien and could be fined in accordance with fines specified in the federal criminal code.

Authorizes a contingency fund of $35 million for use in immigration emergencies such as the 1980 boat-lift from Cuba.

Requires states to verify the status of non-citizens applying for public aid, such as food stamps, welfare programs, public housing and unemployment compensation. Under the law, states will be reimbursed 100 percent for the implementation costs of this provision. However, the Secretaries of the appropriate Departments, such as Agriculture, Health and Human Services, and Labor, could waive this verification rule.

OTHER CHANGES IN THE IMMIGRATION LAW

As indicated earlier, the other changes in the new legislation will be indicated in the following substantive chapters. These changes deal with (1) changes in colonial quota; (2) special immigrants; (3) a visa waiver pilot program for certain visitors; (4) making visas available to nonpreference immigrants. Finally, there is a section of "miscellaneous provisions" dealing with (1) equal treatment of father; (2) suspension of deportation for certain aliens; (3) a "sense" of Congress respecting treatment of Cuban political prisoners; and (4) denial of crew members non-immigrant visa in cases of strikes.

Chapter 2

ADMISSIBLE ALIENS

Every person applying for entry to the United States—other than a U.S. citizen or national—is considered an alien and classified as an immigrant or nonimmigrant. Technically, an immigrant is an alien entering for permanent (or indefinite) residence, but entering aliens are presumed to be immigrants until establishing the right to nonimmigrant status. A nonimmigrant is an alien entering for a temporary, specified or unspecified, period.

It is important for applicants to ascertain the exact "immigrant" or "nonimmigrant" categories to which they belong in order to apply for the proper entry permits. Failure to do so may have far-reaching effects on their own welfare and that of their families.

The immigration laws specify that a valid immigrant or nonimmigrant visa is one *properly* issued to an eligible applicant. Should an alien obtain a document to which he is not entitled, whether by deception or mistake, he may nevertheless be barred from entry on arrival and inspection by the immigration authorities, and even if admitted, is subject to deportation at any time thereafter.

This chapter will describe the classes of aliens eligible for entry and the allotment of visas under the amended law. Documentary requirements and more detailed descriptions will appear in later chapters.

NONIMMIGRANTS

To be classified as a nonimmigrant, an alien must be:

1. A foreign government official or employee, attendant, servant, or personal employee of either; or member of the immediate family of any of the foregoing.

2. A temporary visitor—for business or pleasure.
3. In transit through the United States, or to or from the United Nations Headquarters.
4. A crewman (i.e., seaman or airman).
5. A treaty trader or treaty investor, his spouse or child—if accompanying or following to join him.
6. A student coming to pursue a full course of study at a qualified institution, his spouse or minor child—accompanying or following to join him.
7. A foreign government representative to, or officer or employee of, an international organization; attendant, servant, or personal employee of any of these; or a member of the immediate family of any of the foregoing.
8. A temporary worker: (1) of distinguished merit and ability, coming to perform exceptional services requiring such qualities; or (2) coming to perform skilled or unskilled work where labor shortages exist; or (3) coming as an "industrial trainee."
9. A bona fide representative of foreign press, radio, film, or other information media, coming solely to engage in such vocation, his spouse or minor child—if accompanying or following to join him.
10. An "exchange visitor" (pursuant to the United States Information and Exchange Act of 1948, or as defined under the new class added by the 1965 amendments: a bona fide student, scholar, trainee, teacher, professor, research assistant, specialist, leader in a specialized field of knowledge or skill, or similar person, coming to participate in a program designated by the Secretary of State for the purpose of pursuing such activity); his alien spouse or minor child—if accompanying or following to join him.

11. A Mexican agricultural worker.
12. A "NATO alien," i.e., NATO official; member
    State representative or member of his staff; member
    of the immediate family of any of these; NATO
    "expert," or member of a civilian component,
    accompanying a force entering under the NATO
    Status-of-Forces Agreement, or attached to or
    employed by an Allied Headquarters under the
    Protocol on the Status of International Military
    Headquarters set up under the North Atlantic
    Treaty, or a dependent of any such person; or an
    attendant, servant, or personal employee of any of
    the foregoing, or member of his immediate family.

IMMIGRANTS

Any alien who does not qualify as a nonimmigrant is
presumed to be an immigrant. The terms "quota immigrant" and "nonquota immigrant," however, are no
longer employed. Those subject to numerical limitations
are still divided into preference and nonpreference categories, but the preference categories have been revised.
Replacing "nonquota immigrants" are "special immigrants" and "immediate relatives" (as the classes who
may enter without limitation).

NUMERICAL LIMITATIONS ON ADMISSIBIL-
ITY: The amended law sets an annual over-all limitation
of 170,000 immigrants (exclusive of "special immigrants"
and "immediate relatives") and a quarterly limit of 45,000
for the first three quarters. It revises the preference
categories and prescribes percentage limitations for each
category. Immigrant "refugees" (who receive "conditional
entries" rather than visas) are restricted to 10,200 annually,
and immigrants from individual foreign states to 20,000
(not, however, to reduce any larger existing quota until

July 1, 1968). During the intermediate period, quota numbers unissued or unused in any year are placed in a "pool" available the following year to *preference* immigrants with oversubscribed quotas, and without regard to place of birth (the usual basis of chargeability). Despite this provision, however, the over-all allocation of visas and "conditional entries" may not exceed the previously mentioned annual and quarterly limitations.

QUOTA CHARGEABILITY: Each country and independent governmental unit is treated as a separate foreign state. Quota chargeability is based on the country of birth, except that:

1. A child accompanied by one or both parents may, if necessary to prevent separation from his family, be charged to the country of either accompanying parent who has received, or is qualified to receive, a visa, provided said country's numerical limitation has not been exhausted.
2. An accompanying wife or husband may be charged to the country of the spouse, if necessary to prevent their separation, if the latter has received, or is qualified to receive a visa, and the country's limitation has not been exhausted.
3. An alien born in this country is considered to have been born in the country of which he is a citizen or subject, or, if not a citizen or subject of any country, in the last foreign country in which he resided.
4. An alien born in a country in which neither parent was born or resided at the time of said birth may be charged to the country of either parent.

An immigrant—other than a "special immigrant" or "immediate relative"—born in colony or other dependency of a foreign state, is chargeable to the governing country's limitation, but the number so chargeable may not exceed one percent of such annual limitation.

IMMIGRANTS EXEMPT FROM NUMERICAL LIMITATION: As already noted, the 1965 amendments include certain changes in terminology. Formerly, immigrants admissible without limitation were called "nonquota immigrants." These are replaced by two newly defined classes:

1. *"Immediate Relatives"*
   This class includes children, spouses, and parents (at least 21 years of age) of United States citizens (at least 21 years of age). The term "children" means unmarried persons under 21 years of age.
2. *"Special Immigrants"*
   This class includes:
   A. Natives of independent countries of the Western Hemisphere (which now include Jamaica, Trinidad-Tobago, Guyana, and Barbados—formerly charged to the British sub-quotas), their spouses and children—if accompanying or following to join them, or if the marriage or birth occurred after entry to the principal alien. (Beginning July 1, 1968, admissibility of this category of "special immigrant" will be limited to 120,000 annually (exclusive of those within the category who are also "immediate relatives" and entering as such).
   B. Resident aliens returning from temporary visits abroad.
   C. Former citizens who lost citizenship through marriage, or through service in allied armed forces during World War II.

D. Ministers of religious denominations having bona fide organizations in the United States needing their services, who, for at least two years immediately preceding application for admission, have been continuously and are seeking entry solely for the purpose of carrying on such vocation, and their spouses and children—if accompanying or following to join them.

E. Present or former employees of the United States Government abroad who have served faithfully for at least 15 years, their accompanying spouses and children (provided the principal officer of a Foreign Service establishment has recommended such classification of the applicant in exceptional circumstances and the Secretary of State approves the recommendation and finds the granting of such status to be in the national interest).

IMMIGRANTS SUBJECT TO NUMERICAL LIMITATION: All other immigrants are subject to the numerical ceilings set forth earlier in the chapter. Visas (and "conditional entries" in the case of refugees) are made available in accordance with the following priorities and percentages:

1. *First Preference Category*
Not exceeding 20% of over-all limit of 170,000, first, to unmarried sons and daughters of United States citizens.

2. *Second Preference Category*
Not exceeding 26% of over-all limit, *plus* visas not required for the first preference category, next, to spouses, unmarried sons and daughters of resident aliens.

3. *Third Preference Category*
Not exceeding 10% of over-all limit, next, to
members of the professions and persons of exceptional ability in the sciences or arts.
4. *Fourth Preference Category*
Not exceeding 10% of over-all limit, *plus* visas not
required by the first three preference categories,
next, to married sons and daughters of United
States citizens.
5. *Fifth Preference Category*
Not exceeding 24% of over-all limit, *plus* visas not
required for the first four preference categories,
next, to brothers and sisters of United States
citizens.
6. *Sixth Preference Category*
Not exceeding 10% of over-all limit, next, to skilled
and unskilled workers in short supply.
7. *Seventh Preference Category*
"Conditional entries," not exceeding 6% of over-all
limit, next, to refugees from Communist or
Communist-dominated countries, or countries
within the "general area of the Middle East"
(defined as the area between and including Libya
on the west; Turkey on the north; Pakistan on the
east; and Saudi Arabia and Ethiopa on the south).
Visas, in lieu of, but not exceeding 50% of such
"conditional entries," may be issued to adjust the
status of refugees already here for two years
continuously before applying for such adjustment.
Refugees now entering likewise will have their
status adjusted to that of permanent residents in
two years.
8. *Nonpreference Immigrants*
Unused visas and "conditional entries" from the
preference classes are made available to nonpref-

erence immigrants according to the strict chronological order in which they qualify. Nonpreference status is presumed until an applicant establishes the right to "immediate relative," "special" or preference immigrant status.

The spouses and children, accompanying or following to join preference or nonpreference immigrants, unless otherwise entitled to immigrant status, are accorded the same status and order of consideration as the principal aliens. Visa applicants are considered in the order of their respective categories. Visas for the first six preference categories are issued in the order of filing petitions with the Attorney General. In the relative and "immediate relative" categories, the petition is filed by the citizen or resident alien claiming such status for the beneficiary alien; in the third preference category (members of the professions and persons of exceptional ability in the sciences or arts), by the prospective immigrant or any person on his behalf; and in the sixth preference category (skilled and unskilled workers), by the prospective employer.

Chapter 3

NONIMMIGRANTS: DOCUMENTARY AND OTHER ENTRY REQUIREMENTS

General Requirements

A nonimmigrant generally is required to have:

1. A passport valid for at least six months beyond the initial period for which he has been admitted, and authorizing him to return to the country from which he came or proceed to some other country.
2. A valid nonimmigrant visa or border-crossing identification card.

A "passport" means a travel document issued by an authorized official of the government to which the bearer owes allegiance, showing his origin, identity, and nationality, if any, and valid for entry to a foreign country. It may consist of more than one document so long as, considered together, the documents fulfill these requirements.

A "border-crossing identification card" is a document of identity so designated, issued to an alien lawfully admitted for permanent residence, or to a resident of foreign contiguous territory, by a consular or immigration officer, for the purpose of crossing the borders between the United States and foreign contiguous territory.

A nonimmigrant visa is valid for such period as may be prescribed by the Secretary of State (not exceeding 48 months) on the basis of the reciprocal treatment accorded to United States nationals by the country of which the alien is a national or "stateless" resident. The number of applications for entry for which a visa is valid is also governed by reciprocity. If no visa is required of United States nationals, the visa is valid for 48 months, and unlimited applications for entry. If warranted in individual cases, however, consular officers may issue visas valid for shorter periods, or fewer applications, or restricted to specified ports of entry, or for use on and after a date subsequent to that of issuance.

DOCUMENTARY WAIVERS: Certain classes of nonimmigrants are exempt, either by law, treaty, or administrative waiver, from some or all documentary requirements.

The following classes are exempt by *law or treaty* from *passport, visa, and border-crossing identification card* requirements:

1. Alien members of the United States Armed Forces—in uniform, or bearing documents so identifying them—applying for admission, pursuant to official orders or permit of the Armed Forces.
2. American Indians born in Canada, having at least 50% blood of the American Indian race.
3. Aliens entering the continental United States, or other place under its jurisdiction, from Guam, Puerto Rico, or the Virgin Islands.
4. Armed service personnel of NATO nations, who are signatories of the Status of Forces Agreement, entering pursuant to its provisions; or who are attached to an Allied Headquarters in the United States set up under the North Atlantic Treaty, entering in connection with official duties under the Protocol on the Status of International Military Headquarters.
5. Aliens entering in connection with employment on projects undertaken under the International Boundary and Water Commission treaty between the United States and Mexico.

The following documentary *waivers* have been made by the immigration authorities, with respect to the nonimmigrants specified:

1. *Visas are not required of:*
    A. Canadian nationals, and aliens having a common nationality with Canadian nationals or British subjects in Bermuda, and residing in Canada or Bermuda (also *passports,* except after visits outside the Western Hemisphere).
    B. British subjects residing in, and coming directly from, the Cayman Islands, and presenting certificates relating to criminal record, political associations and affiliations.
    C. British subjects residing in the Bahamas, who satisfy the United States immigration officer at Nassau, prior to or at embarkation, that they are clearly and beyond doubt entitled to admission in all other respects.
    D. British, French, or Netherlands nationals, or nationals of Jamaica, Trinidad-Tobago or Barbados, residing in British, French, or Netherlands territory in the adjacent islands of the Caribbean, or in Trinidad-Tobago, Jamaica or Barbados, and proceeding to Puerto Rico or the Virgin Islands, or to the United States as agricultural workers.
    E. Mexican nationals, who are crewmen on Mexican aircraft authorized to engage in commercial transportation to the United States, or who are coming to the United States as agricultural workers.
2. *Visas and passports are not required of:*
    A. Mexican nationals, who are military or civilian officials or employees of the Mexican national, state or municipal governments, and members of their families; or who have border-crossing cards; or who are coming solely to apply for

Mexican passports or other official documents
at a Mexican consular office on the United
States side of the border.

B. Natives and residents of the Trust Territory to
the Pacific Islands, coming directly therefrom
to the United States.

C. Aliens in immediate, continuous transit through
this country, en route to another, on transportation lines under contact with this country,
insuring direct transit and departure. This
waiver does not apply to citizens (who are also
residents) of Albania, Bulgaria, Communist
China, Cuba, Czechoslovakia, Estonia,
Hungary, Latvia, Lithuania, North Korea,
Vietnam, Outer Mongolia, Poland, Romania,
East Germany, or the Soviet Union. (Foreign
government officials, their families and employees, in immediate transit through this
country, require only unexpired visas and travel
documents valid for entry to a foreign country
for at least 30 days after applying for entry to
this country).

D. Nonimmigrants unable to obtain the required
documents because of unforseen emergency. In
the case of a Cuban national or resident, a visa
waiver is valid only if he is inspected by United
States immigration and health service officials
immediately before departure, and then proceeds directly to the United States.

In addition to these established exemptions, documentary waivers may be made by joint action of consular
and immigration officers in the case of a nonimmigrant
alien:

1. Who resides in a foreign contiguous territory and is

a member of a group or excursion going to the United States under circumstances making timely procurement of a passport and visa impracticable.

2. Whose passport is not valid for the required statutory period, and who is embarking at a place remote from diplomatic or consular offices where it could be revalidated; or whose government does not revalidate passports more than six months prior to, or until actual expiration.

3. Who is well and favorably known at the consular office, and has previously been issued a non-immigrant visa (since expired), and who is going directly to the United States under emergent circumstances precluding timely issuance of a visa.

4. Who is a member of the armed forces of a foreign country on active duty, and a group of such forces making a friendly visit to the United States on behalf of their own government or the United Nations (under advance arrangements with authorities of the United States armed forces). (Such waiver does not apply to citizens or residents of Albania, Bulgaria, Communist, China, Cuba, Czechoslovakia, Estonia, Hungary, Latvia, Lithuania, North Korea, Vietnam, Outer Mongolia, Poland, Romania, East Germany, or the Soviet Union).

5. Who is a landed immigrant in Canada, applying for a visa at a consular office in Canada, and proceeding to the United States under emergent circumstances precluding timely procurement of a passport or Canadian certificate of identity (and whose port and expected date of arrival are known).

6. Who is within the district of a consular office, authorized by the State Department, because of unusual circumstances prevailing in that district, to

join with immigration officers abroad in documentary waivers in specified classes of cases, and whose case falls within one of these classes.

Procedure for Obtaining a Nonimmigrant Visa

Application for a nonimmigrant visa is made at the consulate in the district where the applicant resides, but the consular officer may accept applications from others present in the district if hardship might otherwise result. The application must be executed in person before the consular officer, but the latter has discretionary authority to waive personal appearance in the case of:

1. A child under 10 years of age.
2. Applicants for diplomatic or official visas.
3. Foreign government officials, NATO officials, or Member State representatives and their accompanying official clerical staffs, and members of their immediate families; certain NATO "experts" and civilian components and their dependents; attendants, servants, or personal employees of any of the foregoing, and members of their immediate families.
4. A temporary visitor for business or pleasure—if applying at a post authorized to accept applications by mail.
5. An alien in transit.
6. A temporary worker of distinguished merit and ability.
7. An exchange visitor qualifying as a leader in a specialized field, who is the recipient of a U.S. Government grant; his spouse and children.
8. A representative of a foreign information medium; his spouse and children.

Application is made on Form FS-257 (or FS-247a, in the case of a temporary visitor for business or pleasure whose personal appearance has been waived; or any other case of such waiver, if the consular officer, in his discretion, so decides). For an alien under 16 years of age, or physically incapable of making application, the form is executed by the parent or guardian, or, if there be none, by anyone having legal custody of or a legitimate interest in the applicant.

CONTENTS OF APPLICATION: The application must state the alien's full and true name, date and place of birth, nationality, marital status, purpose and length of intended stay, and include a personal description of the applicant (including height, complexion, color of hair and eyes, and marks of identification, if any) and any other information required for identification or determination of admissibility.

SUPPORTING DOCUMENTS: The consular officer may require any documents considered necessary to determine eligibility. If a document or record cannot be obtained without actual hardship, other than normal delay and inconvenience, other satisfactory evidence may be accepted. The usual requirements are:

1. *Police Certificate*

If the consular officer has reason to believe that the applicant may have a police record, a police certificate—certification by police or other appropriate authorities of what, if anything, their records show concerning the applicant—may be required. This requirement does not apply to:

> A. Foreign government officials and employees, or foreign government representatives to, and employees of international organizations, and

members of the immediate families of any of these.

B. Member State representatives to or officials of NATO, the accompanying official clerical staffs of Member State representatives, and members of their immediate families.

C. Members of certain treaty forces and civilian components connected with NATO, and their dependents.

2. *Photographs*

Three identical photographs, reflecting a reasonable likeness of the applicant at the time submitted, one and one-half inches square, unmounted, without head covering, on a light background, and showing a full front view of the facial features, are required. The reverse of each copy must be signed by the person executing the application, with the full name of the applicant. In the consular officer's discretion, the photograph requirement may be waived for:

A. A foreign government official; foreign government representative to an international organization and his personal employees; member of the immediate family of any of the foregoing.

B. An applicant under 16 years of age.

C. An applicant for a diplomatic or official visa.

D. An applicant whose photograph—still reflecting a reasonable likeness—is on file at the consular office in connection with a previous visa application.

E. A "NATO alien" eligible for discretionary waiver of the personal appearances requirement.

MEDICAL EXAMINATION: An applicant must submit to a medical examination if:

1. Applying for an exchange-visitor visa and intending to remain for more than a brief period of time (unless qualifying as a leader in a specialized field).
2. Applying for a student visa, and intending to remain for more than a brief period.
3. Coming from an area which indicates the advisability of a medical examination.
4. The consular officer has reason to believe that such examination would disclose ineligibility.

The examination is made by immigration service medical officers—at consular offices where these are available; otherwise, by a contract location physician, or physician selected by the applicant from an approved panel.

REGISTRATION AND FINGERPRINTING: Every applicant must be registered; if under 14 years of age, he is registered through his parent or guardian (but must submit to registration and fingerprinting within 30 days after reaching the age of 14). Registration is automatic in the sense that Form FS-257, when properly completed, constitutes the alien's registration card. Formerly, fingerprinting was required of every applicant 14 years of age or more, but the requirement has now been waived in the case of:

1. A foreign government official; foreign government representative to an international organization; officer or employee of such organization, or personal employee of either; or member of the immediate family of any of the foregoing.
2. A national of a country whose government does not require fingerprinting of United States nationals in the same circumstances, who is:

A. A temporary visitor for business or pleasure, or

B. In immediate and continuous transit through the United States, or

C. Entitled to pass in transit to and from the United Nations and his country.

D. A crewman landing temporarily in pursuit of his duties and departing with the plane or vessel on which he came, or on some other craft, or

E. A "treaty" trader or investor, or

F. A bona fide student, qualified for and coming to pursue a full course of study at a qualified institution, or his alien spouse or minor child—if accompanying or following to join him, or

G. A temporary worker (1) of distinguished merit and ability, or (2) coming to perform skilled or unskilled labor, or (3) coming as an industrial trainee, or

H. A bona fide representative of a foreign press, radio, film, or other information medium, coming solely to engage in such vocation, or his spouse or child—if accompanying or following to join him.

I. A bona fide student, scholar, trainee, teacher, professor, research assistant, specialist, or leader in a field of specialized knowledge or skill, or other person of similar description, coming temporarily to participate in a program designated by the Secretary of State for the purpose of pursuing some such activity (a member of this class is known as an "exchange visitor"); or

J. A "NATO alien"—as previously described.

ISSUANCE OF VISA: Approval of the application is indicated by a stamp placed in the nonimmigrant's passport and signed by the consular officer as in the following specimen:

No. ....

(Title of office)

(SEAL)   (Location)

NONIMMIGRANT VISA

Classification: ....

Date: ....

Valid if presented before ....

for .... applications for admission into the United States.

Issued to ....

....

....

(Name and title of consular officer)

Diplomatic and official visas are in the same form, except that they bear the title "Diplomatic" or "Official." In certain cases, the stamp is not placed in the passport, but on such form as prescribed by the State Department, with a notation indicating which of the following excepted classes of cases is involved:

1. Where the passport was issued by a government having no formal diplomatic relations with the United States (in such cases, however, the Department may specifically authorize placing the stamp in the passport).
2. Where the passport provides insufficient space for the stamp.
3. Where the passport requirement has been waived.
4. Other cases as authorized by the Department.

FEES: Visa fees are generally based on reciprocity, i.e., correspond to the fee, if any, charged to an American national by the country of which the applicant is a national. However, there is no fee for foreign government officials, foreign government representatives to international organizations, aliens passing in transit to and from the United Nations Headquarters, "NATO aliens," and nonimmigrants issued diplomatic visas.

PERIOD OF VALIDITY: A nonimmigrant visa is valid for such period as may be prescribed by the Secretary of State on the basis, so far as practicable, of reciprocity of treatment accorded American nationals in the same circumstances, but not, in any case, to exceed 48 months. The number of applications for admission permissible during the period of the visa's validity is also determined on the basis of reciprocity. If the alien's government requires no visa of American nationals, or the alien is "stateless" the visa is valid for the full 48 months and unlimited applications for entry.

REVALIDATION: A nonimmigrant visa may, in the consular officer's discretion, be revalidated any number of times (which do not, in the aggregate, extend its validity over 48 months from the date of original issuance, except in the case of crewman (who require certification from their carriers of continued employment, or personal evidence of continued "crewman" status) or temporary visitors for business or pleasure). The re-validated visa must bear the same classification as the original, and may be issued only if:

(1) The alien's nationality is the same.
(2) The visa is about to expire, has expired, or become invalid by exhaustion of the specified number of applications for admission.
(3) Application for revalidation is made within one year of expiration of the original or any previous revalidation of the visa, and
(4) The consular officer is satisfied that the applicant is a bona fide nonimmigrant and otherwise eligible for a nonimmigrant visa.

Revalidation is effected by placing the visa stamp in the alien's passport, inserting the word "REVALIDATED" in its upper margin, and transferring all pertinent data from the original to the revalidated visa. Re-execution of Form FS-257 is not required, but a notation of revalidation is entered on the reverse of the original. If revalidation is not made at the issuing office, appropriate notification is given to that office. The fee is the same as for issuance, but a visa issued for a shorter period, or fewer applications for entry than permitted by reciprocity may be revalidated for the remaining period and permissible number of applications without an additional fee. Any visa, of course, becomes invalid if the passport expires. A visa may, however, be transferred to a new passport, except where the passport containing the original visa has been lost or stolen, provided the new passport indicates that the alien has the same nationality as when the visa was issued. The word "Transferred" is inserted on the upper margin of the visa stamp, and a notation of the transfer made on the reverse of Form FS-257 on file at the original issuing office. There is no fee for the transfer.

REFUSAL OF VISA: No person will be issued a nonimmigrant visa who does not first satisfy the consular officer that:

1. He is actually not an immigrant, i.e., does not really have the intention of coming to the United States for permanent residence, or for a longer period than permitted.
2. He will not be barred from admission for any of the reasons specified in Chapter 5, applicable to non-immigrants, such as being a criminal, subversive, or immoral person (this does not apply to a foreign government official, or member of his immediate family, unless the President of the United States

directs that he be barred notwithstanding, or a foreign government official in transit to and from the United Nations Headquarters, unless he is excludable for reasons of security).

However, irrespective of the grounds of excludability of aliens specified in Chapter 5, no nonimmigrant will be refused a visa or denied admission to this country solely on the ground that he is:

1. Unable to read and understand any language.
2. A polygamist or person who advocates that practice.
3. A person afflicted with a physical defect or disease, other than a dangerous, contagious disease, affecting his ability to earn a living, or who, in the opinion of the consular or immigration authorities, might become a public charge for any other reason, *provided* that he posts a bond or other undertaking insuring that he will not become such a charge (with the consent of the immigration authorities); or
4. A person seeking admission from foreign contiguous territories or adjacent islands, without having resided there for at least two years after arriving there, and coming to this country on a transportation line which has not complied with certain requirements placed on it by the immigration law (with certain exceptions, set forth in detail in Chapter 5).

If an applicant fails to execute Form FS-257 after being informed of a ground of ineligibility, the visa is considered refused. Where possible however, this form should be executed before a refusal is recorded. The case is reviewed by the principal consular officer or a designated alternate. If the applicant indicates an intention to obtain additional evidence, which may overcome the grounds of ineligibility, such review may be deferred for a period not exceeding 120 days. If the reviewing officer does not concur in the refusal, he either assumes responsibility for the case himself, or refers it to the State Department for an advisory opinion. The Department, on its own initiative, may require submission to it for review of individual or specified classes of cases and for the rendering of an advisory opinion. Its interpretations of law, but not its application to the facts, are binding on the consular officer. If he contemplates action contrary to the advisory opinion, he resubmits the case to the Department with an explanation of the proposed action.

REVOCATION AND INVALIDATION: A nonimmigrant visa may be *revoked as of the date issued* if the consular officer learns that it was procured by fraud, deceit, concealment, or other unlawful means, or that the applicant was ineligible to receive it when it was issued; it may be *invalidated as of the date such action is taken* if the consular officer finds that the bearer *has become ineligible* for a visa. If practicable, the bearer is notified of the contemplated action, afforded an opportunity to show cause why it should not be taken, and requested to present the travel document containing the visa. A visa may be revoked or invalidated even though the alien is already in this country; and failure to present a visa for cancellation does not, of course, affect the validity of a revocation. Cancellation is effected by plainly writing "Revoked" or "Invalidated" across the face of the visa. Notice of revocation or invalidation is transmitted to the issuing office and, together with a full report of the facts, to the State Department for forwarding to the Immigration and Naturalization Service (but not where cancellation occurs before the alien's departure for the United States, except in the cases of foreign government officials, or representatives to international organizations, aliens in transit to United Nations Headquarters, and those with NATO, diplomatic, or official visas).

If the visa is not surrendered for cancellation, notice of revocation or invalidation is also given the carrier or transportation line that the alien intends to use.

Any evidence indicating that revocation or invalidation was unwarranted may be submitted to, and must be considered by, the consular officer. If he determines that the action taken was improper, the visa is reinstated.

Conditions of Admission and Stay

The period of a visa's validity is the time during which it may be used to apply for admission, and should not be confused with the period of stay authorized when an application is granted. The latter is determined, within limits set by regulations, by the admitting officer on the basis of the purpose of the proposed entry. The permissible periods of admission for the respective classes of non-immigrants are discussed later in the chapter.

Every applicant for entry must:

1. Establish his admissibility, or a waiver of any ground for exclusion.
2. Present a valid passport and visa, unless either or both have been waived.
3. Agree to abide by all conditions of admission, including maintenance of status, and to depart at expiration of the period authorized, or termination of his nonimmigrant status.
4. To post a bond for not less than $500 insuring maintenance of status and timely departure—if required by immigration authorities.

EXTENSION OF STAY: Nonimmigrants whose periods of admission have not expired may, with certain exceptions, apply for extensions. This is done on Form

1-539, except in the case of "exchange visitors" who use Form DSP-66 (Certificate of Eligibility for Exchange-Visitor Status). If the application is denied, there is no appeal. The exceptions are:

1. Crewmen, and nonimmigrants in transit to and from the United Nations Headquarters, who are ineligible for extensions.
2. Foreign government officials, and representatives to international organizations; officers and employees of such organizations; members of the immediate families of the foregoing classes. Such persons do not require extensions so long as they are recognized as members of these classes by the Secretary of State.
3. Mexican agricultural workers, who are admitted for a maximum period of six months.

The application must be accompanied by a passport valid for six months beyond the period for which the application is made; the entry permit; and a fee payable by check or money order to "Immigration and Naturalization Service, Department of Justice." Students, and employees of foreign government officials and international organization personnel, are exempt from the fee. Additional documents or statements required of special classes of nonimmigrants are described under the appropriate headings later in the chapter.

A separate application is required for each applicant for extension, except that a child under 14 years of age may be included in the application of the parent, and without an additional fee.

The application must contain: a complete description of the applicant; conditions on which he was admitted to this country; his manner of compliance therewith; and the reasons for his inability to depart on the date originally fixed, or as later extended.

TEMPORARY ADMISSION OF EXCLUDABLE ALIENS: A prospective nonimmigrant who is ineligible for a visa, or, though possessing proper documents, excludable on any ground specified in Chapter 5, other than reasons of security or public interest, may nevertheless be admitted temporarily in the discretion of the Attorney General. When a visa is not required, application is made on Form 1-192, to the district director of the intended port of entry. If inadmissibility is due to past or present membership in, or affiliation with, a Communist or other totalitarian party or organization, there must be attached a statement of such membership or affiliation; whether the applicant held any office in such organization; and whether such affiliation was voluntary or involuntary, and if the latter, the basis of such claim. If inadmissible because of disease, the applicant must attach a statement describing the disease; and, if entry is sought for treatment, that satisfactory treatment cannot be obtained outside of the United States, that arrangements for treatment have been completed, including a statement as to financial arrangements for payment; and that a bond will be given if required.

If inadmissibility is based on conviction of crime, the statement must designate each such offense; the date and place of commission, conviction, and sentence or other judgment of the court; and be supplemented by official records concerning any commutation, parole, probation, or pardon. If the alien has not previously applied for the exercise of discretionary admission, he may do so on arrival at the port of entry, *provided* he can establish that he was unaware of the ground of inadmissibility before departure, and could not have learned of it by using reasonable diligence, and *also provided* that he has, or has been granted a waiver of appropriate entry documents (application for waiver of documents is made on Form 1-193 upon payment of a fee plus costs of communication between the port of entry and Central Office of the Immigration and Naturalization Service).

The applicant is notified of the decision, and, if adverse, of the reasons, and the right of appeal (within 15 days after mailing of such notification, to the Board of Immigration Appeals). A denial of the application is also no bar to a renewed application before a "special inquiry officer." The regulations specify certain cases where the decision of a special inquiry officer is appealable, and others where it is not. If appealable, either the applicant or district director may appeal an adverse decision.

In cases where a visa is required, the consular officer may, on his own initiative, and must, if requested by the Secretary of State, submit a report as to the possible issuance of a visa to the prospective entrant to the State Department for possible transmission to the Attorney General. In specified categories of cases, a consular officer may recommend to designated immigration officers the temporary admission of an alien. Where a recommendation is made by a consular officer or other State Department official, no application or fee is required.

ALIENS PREVIOUSLY DEPORTED, REMOVED, OR WHO HAVE DEPARTED AT GOVERNMENT EXPENSE: A nonimmigrant who has been the subject of a previous immigration proceeding may apply for permission to reapply for admission to the United States by submitting an application to the appropriate consular officer. (An immigrant applies to immigration authorities on Form 1-212. If abroad, he submits the application to the district director having jurisdiction over the place of the prior proceedings or to the immigration officer having jurisdiction over his place of residence. If applying at the port of entry, he submits the application to the district director having jurisdiction over that port. If in the United States, and *also applying concurrently* for an adjustment of status, he submits the application to the district director having jurisdiction over that proceeding, unless it is pending before a special inquiry officer, in which case he submits the application to the district director having jurisdiction over his place of residence).

The application must include a statement of facts showing:

1. That unusual hardship would result to persons lawfully in the United States if the application were denied, or

2. That there is a need for the applicant's services in the United States, or

3. That he is a bona fide crewman with no means of earning a livelihood except by following his calling, which requires him to come to the United States, or

4. That he must enter the United States frequently over the international land border to buy the necessities of life, or in connection with a business in which he is engaged, or for some other urgent reason.

If the application is denied, an appeal may be taken within 15 days after mailing of notification of the decision. (A nonimmigrant has no right to appeal).

PAROLE OF NONIMMIGRANTS INTO THE UNITED STATES: For urgent reasons, or reasons considered strictly in the public interest, an alien applying for admission, but found excludable and not entitled to discretionary permission to enter temporarily, may still be allowed to enter under *parole,* upon any conditions (including the furnishing of a bond on Form 1-352) considered appropriate by the immigration authorities.

Such a situation may occur, for example, where an alien is in need of immediate medical attention, or is required as a witness in a court of law.

Parole is not regarded as an admission into the United States, and when it is determined that its purpose has been served, the alien will be treated in the same manner as any other applicant for admission to this country.

The Special Classes of Nonimmigrants

Every alien claiming nonimmigrant status must establish his qualification for the particular category in which he claims membership, to the satisfaction of both the consular officer (when applying for a visa) and the immigration officer examining him upon arrival at a port of entry in this country. The individual classifications available to persons claiming nonimmigrant status are as follows:

A. *Foreign Government Officials*
This group includes accredited officials or employees of a foreign government recognized "de jure" (by law) by the United States Government and acceptable to the President or Secretary of State. It refers specifically to the following person:

1. Ambassadors, public ministers, or career diplomatic or consular officers and members of their immediate families.

2. Other foreign government officials and employees and members of their immediate families—on a basis of reciprocity, i.e., provided U.S. nationals having the same status are accorded similar treatment by their governments.

3. Attendants, servants, and personal employees of the groups just described, and their immediate families—also on a basis of reciprocity.

DEFINITIONS: It is well at this point to note the specific meanings and limitationss of certain descriptive terms as used in the immigration laws:

1. An "accredited official" means an alien holding an official position, other than honorary, who possesses a travel document showing that he is coming to or through the United States to transact official business for his government and that he is a national of the government he serves. If not such a national, he may be classified as a *temporary visitor* or an *alien in transit,* as explained later.

2. "Immediate family" includes close relatives who are members of the immediate family by virtue of blood, marriage, or adoption, and who will reside regularly in the household of the person from whom they derive their status.

3. "Attendants" are aliens paid from the public funds of the foreign government employing them and to which they owe allegiance; and who are preceding, accompanying, following to join the official or employee to whom they owe a duty or service, whatever its nature. The term also includes an attendant who is a member of the armed forces of the foreign government to whom both master and attendant owe allegiance.

4. "Servants" and "personal employees" include aliens who are employed in domestic or personal capacities by a foreign government official or employee, and paid from the private funds of the latter; and who seek entry to this country solely for the purpose of serving their employer.

Special Limitations

Generally, no alien will be accorded the privileges of a nonimmigrant within the foreign official class if the facts in his particular case do not clearly place him within this group. Thus, an official of a foreign government not legally recognized by the United States may not be classified as a nonimmigrant foreign government official. If otherwise qualified for admission, however, he may be classified as a temporary visitor, transit alien, or member of some other appropriate category.

An official coming on *personal* business must apply for a visa as a temporary visitor for business (explained later). An alien regularly and professionally employed as a courier by the government to which he owes allegiance, or an official coming to this country in this capacity is eligible for an official visa, but if holding no official position or not a national of such country, he must apply for a visitor's visa. However, an alien seeking entry as a foreign government representative to an international organization and also as a foreign government official, on official business, may be issued a visa as a member of the latter class, if otherwise qualified.

Aliens claiming eligibility for classification as foreign government officials may be required by the consular officer to submit evidence of their asserted status, as well as details of the manner and destination of their journey to and through the United States.

CONDITIONS OF ADMISSION AND STAY: The importance of obtaining a properly issued "official" visa lies in the fact that it constitutes *conclusive* evidence of its bearer's status, unless, in exceptional circumstances, an immigration officer is otherwise advised by higher immigration authorities after consultation with the State Department. In such event, the foreign official may be held for further inquiry. Ordinarily, however, persons in this category are not excludable for the reasons specified in Chapter 5, provided they are acceptable to the President and Secretary of State.

Persons in this category may be admitted for indefinite periods so long as recognized by the State Department as members of this class. However, attendants, servants, personal employees, and members of their immediate families, are admitted initially, and granted extensions in increments of not more than one year. While the officials and members of their immediate families, who are admitted indefinitely, are not required to post an undertaking, attendants, servants, and employees may be called upon, as a condition of entry, to post a bond or other assurance of departure upon expiration of their authorized period of stay or termination of their status.

If a foreign government official or employee (designated in the first two subdivisions described) becomes ineligible to remain in this country in such official status, each alien member of his family, attendant, servant, or personal employee, or member of the immediate family of any of the latter, is also treated as having failed to maintain his status.

An application for an extension of stay by an attendant, servant, or personal employee is made on Form 1-539, filed with the nearest immigration office and accompanied by a written statement from the employing official describing the applicant's current and intended employment.

B. *Temporary Visitors*

An alien seeking a visitor's visa must specifically establish that:

1. He has a residence in a foreign country which he has no intention of abandoning.

2. He is not classifiable as an alien coming to study, or to perform skilled or unskilled labor, or as a representative of a foreign information medium.

3. He is proceeding to this country temporarily as a visitor for business or pleasure.

4. He intends in good faith to depart from the United States upon expiration of his authorized period of stay.

5. He has a valid foreign visa or other permit to enter some foreign country when his stay in this country has expired.

6. He has made adequate financial arrangements to carry out the purpose of his sojourn in this country.

DEFINITIONS: "Business" refers to legitimate activity of a professional or commercial character, but does not include employment or labor for hire. A nonimmigrant coming in the latter capacity must apply for a "temporary worker's" visa. However, an alien of distinguished merit and ability coming to perform temporary services requiring such qualifications may be classified as a temporary visitor for business.

"Pleasure" refers to the activities of an alien coming as a tourist, or to visit with relatives or friends, or for reasons of health, amusement, or education (other than a specific activity which would classify him as a "student," "exchange visitor," or specialist coming to engage in a program sponsored by the Secretary of State). No alien seeking admission as a student or for prearranged employment may be considered a temporary visitor for pleasure except by special permission of the consular and immigration authorities.

The classification symbol of a temporary visitor for business is "B-1," while that of a visitor for pleasure is designated "B-2."

Note: The personal servant or personal employee of a temporary visitor (including a chauffeur, valet, lady's maid, nursemaid, and a private or social secretary; but not a domestic or household servant, such as a butler, cook, general maid, charwoman, or gardner) may, if otherwise qualified, be considered a visitor for business, provided:

1. Such person is accompanying the employer; or

2. Is accompanying a U.S. citizen employer, who has a residence or is stationed abroad, and who is planning to visit in the United States temporarily for business or pleasure.

However, the consular officer must be satisfied that such accompanying alien is a bona fide personal servant and will be willing and able to leave this country not later than the accompanied employer.

CONDITIONS OF ADMISSION AND STAY: A temporary visitor for business or pleasure may be admitted initially for a period of not more than six months. Extensions of stay are likewise limited to six months each. However, if such alien is the spouse or child of a nonimmigrant admitted as a temporary worker of exceptional merit and ability or as one coming to perform skilled or unskilled labor, the period of admission or extension is one year. A bond may be required if the admitting immigration officer considers one necessary to insure compliance with the terms of admission, or timely departure. If no previous undertaking has been posted, one may be required at the time of application for an extension. The visitor may not accept any employment during his stay.

C. *Transient Aliens*
An alien applying for immediate and continuous transit through the United States must establish:

1. That he is admissible.

2. That he seeks to enter the United States temporarily and solely for the purpose of proceeding in immediate and continuous transit through his country en route to a specific foreign destination, or that he qualifies as a person entitled to pass in transit to and from the United Nations Headquarters District by treaty arrangement.

3. That he is in possession of a ticket or other assurance

of transportation to his destination, or, if coming to join an aircraft or vessel, that it will depart directly within five calendar days (and, if a vessel, that he has or then applies for Form 1-184 (permanent landing permit and identification card).

4. That he has sufficient funds to enable him to carry out the purpose of his transit journey or enough money otherwise available for that purpose.

5. That he holds a valid foreign visa or other entry permit if required by the country of destination. (Application for direct transit without a visa (except from one part of contiguous foreign territory to another) may be made at certain ports of entry specified in the regulations).

6. That he intends in good faith, and will be able, to depart from this country at expiration of the period for which he is permitted to enter, and

7. That he is not ineligible for a nonimmigrant visa for any of the reasons specified in Chapter 5.

Note: The personal servant or personal employee, such as a chauffeur, valet, lady's maid, nursemaid, or private or social secretary, accompanying the employer in immediate and continuous transit, may, if otherwise qualified, obtain a transit alien's visa. This does not include a domestic or household servant, such as a butler, cook, general maid, charwoman, or gardener.

CONDITIONS OF ADMISSION AND STAY: A transit alien may be admitted for any period of time not in excess of 29 days. An alien whose visa is limited to transit to and from the United Nations Headquarters District must proceed directly to its "immediate vicinity" (an area within a 25 mile radius of Columbus Circle, New York City), and remain there continuously during this sojourn in this country, leaving only when departing from the country.

D. *Crewmen*

No alien crewman may enter the United States without a Form 1-184 (permanent landing permit and identification card) issued by the immigration port authorities, except a Canadian or British citizen crewman on a vessel plying between the United States and Canada; a crewman on a vessel which does not ordinarily call at U.S. ports; a crewman with less than one year's sea service; or a crewman making his first application for Form 1-184, who is otherwise admissible.

An immigration examination is not required of crewmen aboard a Great Lakes vessel of U.S. registry, arriving at a U.S. port, who have previously been examined and admitted as members of the same crew of the same vessel or any other vessel of the same company during the current calendar year; or who are either British or Canadian citizens aboard a Great Lakes vessel of Canadian or British registry, arriving at a U.S. port for less than 20 days, who have previously been examined and admitted as members of the same crew of the same or any other vessel of the same company during the current calendar year, or are in possession of Form 1-95 (conditional landing permit) issued in the same calendar year as members of the same crew, and who do not require landing privileges in the United States beyond the time the vessel will be in port, and who will depart therewith for Canada.

CREW-LISTS: The owner, master, commanding officer, agent, or consignee of an incoming vessel must present to the immigration officer at the port of arrival a Form FI-418 (Passenger List-Crew List) containing the names of all crewmen (the statute says: "all alien crewmen," while the regulations specify "all crewmen aboard" (which would include citizens). In the case of incoming *aircraft* (unless coming directly from a point of origin in

Canada, in which case a crew-list is unnecessary), the form used is Customs Form 7507 (General Declaration) or the International Civil Aviation Organization General Declaration.

A crewman of a fishing vessel having its home port or operating base in the United States is classifiable as an immigrant. Aliens employed aboard a vessel or aircraft in capacities not ordinarily associated with or required for normal operation and service are considered as passengers. The same is true of crewmen in excess of the number normally required for a crew.

CONDITIONS OF ADMISSION AND STAY: A bona fide nonimmigrant crewman, not otherwise excludable for any reason specified in Chapter 5, will be allowed to land on the following conditions:

1. If the immigration officer is satisfied that the crewman intends to leave on the same vessel or craft, he may remain for the same period of time that such vessel or craft is in port, but not longer than 29 days (crewmen in this class are designated "D-1").

2. If the immigration officer is satisfied that the crewman intends to leave on some other vessel or aircraft within the time allowed, he may remain for 29 days (such crewmen are designated "D-2").

A crewman permitted to land under the first condition may not be paid off and discharged from his vessel without special permission of the Immigration and Naturalization Service. A landing permit under the second condition, however, is regarded as an automatic consent to discharge.

A crewman seeking admission other than as a bona fide seaman or airman must comply with all requirements for entry as a passenger.

In no event will a crewman be permitted an extension of stay beyond 29 days from the date of first temporary landing except under the most emergent and extra-ordinary conditions. The law makes special provision for the landing and treatment of crewmen who are disabled and require hospitalization.

VIOLATION OF LANDING PERMIT: Generally the conditions of a crewman's permit to land are considered violated if:

1. It is determined that he is not a bona fide crewman. He is not a bona fide crewman if (a) he violates the terms of his admission, (b) shows in any way an intention to violate such terms, (c) engages in any activity inconsistent with his status as a crewman, or (d) was not entitled to land as crewman at the time of landing.

2. He does not intend to depart on the vessel or aircraft on which he came (if admitted under the first condition) or on some other vessel or aircraft (if admitted under the second condition). Such violation may be indicated (a) by any evidence, oral or in writing, or any conduct showing that he does not intend to leave, (b) if he is found at such a distance from the port of landing that it will be impossible for him to depart on time, (c) if by reason of his own conduct it will be impossible for him to leave on the same or some other craft, according to the terms of his permit, or (d) if he remains in the United States after expiration of the time for which he was permitted to land.

In addition to deportation, the law provides criminal penalties for any alien crewman who wilfully remains in the United States for a longer period than permitted, making it a misdeameanor punishable by a fine up to $500, imprisonment up to six months, or both. If detained for prosecution or confined in a penal or mental institution at the time he is found to be violating the terms of his landing permit, a crewman will not be returned to his vessel until released. If it has departed by that time, he may be deported on another ship of the same transportation line if practicable; if not, in any other manner, at the expense of the said line. A crewman admitted under the first condition, and later deported, has no right to a formal hearing allowed other nonimmigrants, and no right to appeal from the decision revoking his landing permit.

E. *Treaty Traders and Investors*

Aliens in this class, applying for nonimmigrant visas, must satisfy both consular and immigration authorities that they are entitled to enter the United States:

1. As *treaty traders,* i.e., solely to carry on substantial trade, principally between the United States and the countries of which they are nationals, or the operations of enterprises in which they have invested, or are actively in the process of investing substantial amounts of capital, under, and in pursuance of, treaties of commerce and navigation between the United States and their own governments. They must also establish that they are not ineligible for visas or admission for any of the reasons specified in Chapter 5.

Such visas are also available to their spouses and children, accompanying or following to join them. The nationality of a spouse or child is immaterial for this purpose.

DEFINITIONS: The term "national", in this context, means a citizen or subject of a country having, at the time of application for a visa and entry, a treaty of "commerce and navigation" with the United States. "Trade" means trade of a substantial nature, international in scope, carried on by the alien either in his own behalf or as an agent of a foreign person or organization so engaged, and carried on principally between the United States and the country of which the alien is a national. Consideration is given to conditions in his own government affecting his ability to carry on such substantial trade with this country.

COUNTRIES WITH TREATIES OF COMMERCE AND NAVIGATION WITH THE U.S.

Treaties of commerce and navigation providing for trade and investment (E-1 and E-2 status) exist with the following countries:

Argentina
Austria
Belgium
China
Colombia
Costa Rica
Ethiopia
France
Germany
Honduras
Iran
Italy
Japan
Korea
Liberia
Luxembourg

Netherlands
Nicaragua
Norway
Oman
Pakistan
Paraguay
Philippines
Spain
Suriname
Switzerland
Thailand
Togo
United Kingdom
Vietnam
Yugoslavia

Treaties of commerce and navigation conferring only E-1 treaty-trader status exist with the following countries:

Bolivia
Brunei
Denmark
Estonia
Finland

Greece
Ireland
Israel
Latvia
Turkey

Over the years, certain special conditions have come to be a part of the treaties mentioned above.

1. Iran. Still in effect despite lack of diplomatic relations.
2. Vietnam. Currently not in effect.
3. Korea. South Korea only.
4. Germany. West Germany and West Berlin only.
5. Latvia and Estonia. A throwback to the "cold-war" era; little current application.
6. United Kingdom. Only for British nationals "normally resident" in the U.K.; no "landed immigrants" (permanent residents) of Canada, Hong Kong, or other countries.
7. China. Taiwan only.
8. Nicaragua. On May 1, 1985, the United States moved to terminate the treaty with Nicaragua by giving one-year notice under the treaty. The termination becomes effective on May 1, 1986; the status of current E visa holders from Nicaragua after termination is presently unclear. Interested parties should contact the State Department to confirm termination of the treaty on May 1, 1986, and to clarify the status of current visa holders.

EXPLANATION: To qualify as a *treaty trader,* the alien must establish that:

1. He is coming to carry on substantial trade with this country as defined in the foregoing paragraph. As supporting evidence, he may be required to submit bank statements, invoices, and correspondence from persons (or organizations) with whom he has, or will have, commercial relations.

2. He intends in good faith, and will be able, to depart when either his particular status or the treaty under which he is operating terminates.

3. His employer, if any, will be a foreign person or organization, and that he will be engaged in supervisory or executive duties, or, if employed in a lesser capacity, that he has special qualifications making his services

essential to the efficient operations of his employer (an alien employed solely as a laborer or other manual worker is ineligible for treaty trader classification).

To qualify as a *treaty investor,* the alien must establish that:

1. He is coming for the sole purpose of investing a substantial amount of capital pursuant to a treaty of commerce and navigation negotiated after June 27, 1952 (or has so invested).

2. The enterprise in which he has, or intends to make, an investment is actual, or in the process of formation, and not merely a fictitious paper operation.

3. He is not seeking a nonimmigrant visa to evade quota or other restrictions applicable to immigrants.

4. He intends in good faith, and will be able, to depart upon termination of his status or of the treaty under which he operates.

CONDITIONS OF ADMISSION AND STAY: Members of this class are admitted initially for periods not exceeding one year. Extensions of stay are granted in increments not exceeding one year. Treaty merchants admitted before July 1, 1924 were admitted for permanent residence. Treaty traders entering between July 1, 1924 and December 24, 1952 were admitted without time limitation, but must file annual reports (on Form 1-126) showing maintenance of status. There is no fee, and they are not required to file Form 1-539 (application for extension of stay). Those admitted after December 24, 1952 must file both forms.

F. *Students*
To qualify as a nonimmigrant student, an alien must establish that he:

1. Has a residence in a foreign country which he has no intention of abandoning.

2. Is a bona fide student qualified to pursue, and seeking to enter the United States temporarily and solely for the purpose of pursuing, a full course of study at an established institution of learning or recognized place of study or research.

3. Has sufficient funds to cover his expenses or that other arrangements have been made to provide for them.

4. Has sufficient scholastic preparation and knowledge of the English language to enable him to undertake a full course of study in the institution which has accepted him; or, if not so qualified, the institution must be equipped to offer and be ready to accept him for a full program of study in a language with which he is familiar, or special arrangements must have been made for tutoring him in English. If coming to study English exclusively, the school must be equipped to furnish and have accepted him expressly for a full course in the English language, even though no credits are given for such study. (In such cases, a copy of the letter of the school setting forth the special arrangements must be attached to the visa issued by the consul).

5. Intends in good faith, and will be ready and able to leave the United States when his status has terminated.

6. Is not eligible for admission on any ground specified in Chapter 5.

A nonimmigrant student must first be accepted and have made definite arrangements to enter an institution of learning or recognized place of study or research. He must agree not to attend any other than the authorized institution unless first granted permission by the Immigration and Naturalization Service. Pursuance of a full course of study requires that the student carry courses consisting of at least 12 semester hours as an undergraduate, or a full program generally required for a graduate student, or at an American institute of research recognized by the Attorney General. An "approved" educational institution is one so designated by the Attorney General after consultation with the Office of Education of the United States after fulfilling certain requirements. One specified condition is that the institution agree to report to the Attorney General the termination of attendance of each nonimmigrant alien student. Failure to do so promptly is a cause for withdrawal of approval.

A nonimmigrant student must also file (and his spouse or child, accompanying or following to join him, must present) Form 1-20 (Certificate of Eligibility for Non-immigrant "F-1" Student Status). It is filled out by the student and school in which he is enrolled, stating that he is taking a full course of study, and indicating the expiration date of his stay as shown on his Form 1-94 (Arrival-Departure Record).

CONDITIONS OF ADMISSION AND STAY: A member of this class is admitted initially for a period not to exceed one year and may be granted extensions not exceeding one year each. Ordinarily he may not engage in employment, whether for wages, board or lodging, but if unable to meet necessary expenses, he may apply at the nearest office of the Immigration and Naturalization Service, on Form 1-538, for permission to engage in, or continue, employment, provided it will not displace a United States resident. If an extension of stay is necessary, this form will be accepted in lieu of Form 1-539. If employment for practical training is required or recommended by the institution, the student may be permitted to engage in such employment for a six-month period, subject to extension for two additional such periods if the school and training agency certify that such training cannot be completed in less time. If an institution has alternate work-study courses the student may participate in these without applying on Form 1-538. A student may also engage in "on-campus" employment that is part of his academic program and related to it, if it will not displace a United States resident. No permission is required for such employment.

G. *Foreign Government Representatives to and Employees of International Organizations*

An alien applying for a nonimmigrant visa in this category must be one of the following:

1. A designated principal resident representative of a foreign government (legally recognized by the United States) to an international organization of which his country is a member.

2. An accredited resident member of his staff.

3. An accredited representative (other than the principal resident representative) of a foreign government (legally recognized by this country) to an international organization of which his country is a member.

4. An accredited representative of a foreign government (*not* legally recognized by the United States) to an international organization of which his country is a member.

5. An accredited representative of a foreign government (legally recognized by the United States) to an international organization of which his country is *not* a member.

6. An accredited representative of a foreign government (*not* legally recognized by this country) to an international organization of which his country is *not* a member.

7. An officer or employee of an international organization.

8. An attendant, servant, or personal employee of a representative, official, or employee in any of the aforementioned groups.

9. A member of the immediate family of any member of the aforementioned groups.

To qualify for nonimmigrant status in this class, the alien claiming such status must be travelling to, or in transit through, the United States solely on official business connected with such an international organization. The international organization must be one designated by the President of the United States as entitled to enjoy the privileges, exemptions, and immunities conferred by the International Organization Immunities Act of 1945. These include the privileges and immunities accorded to officials and employees of foreign governments with respect to entry and departure, alien registration and fingerprinting, registration as foreign agents, and immunity from suit and legal process for acts done in an official capacity (unless waived by the foreign government or international organization).

DEFINITIONS: A member of the "immediate family" of an alien in this class is any close relative by reason of blood, marriage, or adoption, who will reside regularly in the household of such principal alien from whom he derives his nonimmigrant status. An "attendant" is one who is paid from the public funds of the foreign government to which he owes allegiance, or the funds of the international organization, and who is accompanying or following to join the principal alien to whom he owes a duty or service. A "servant" or "personal employee" is one employed in a personal or domestic capacity by the principal alien, paid from the private funds of the latter, and entering this country solely for the purpose of such employment.

Any evidence required to establish qualification for a visa in this category, including information respecting the means and destination of the journey, may be demanded by the consular officer. Verification of the alien's status as a foreign government representative (etc.) may be obtained through his foreign office or through the international organization. If the purpose of travel be personal, or for private business or pleasure, the alien must apply for an appropriate entry permit for such purpose, irrespective of his position as a foreign government representative (etc.). However, as noted earlier, if an alien seeks entry both as a foreign government official and foreign government representative to an international organization, he will be granted a visa appropriate to the former.

CONDITIONS OF ADMISSION AND STAY: Representatives to, and officials and employees of, international organizations are admitted indefinitely so long as they continue to be recognized by the Secretary of State. This entails notification to, and tripartite acceptance by, the United States, the foreign government to which the alien owes allegiance, and the international organization.

Attendants, servants, personal employees, and their families, however, are admitted initially for not longer than one year, and may be required to furnish bonds. Furthermore, if the principal alien loses his status, the derivative status of such employees and their families also ceases.

If an attendant, servant, or personal employee requires an extension of stay (which may also be granted in increments of not over one year), he must attach to his application a written statement from his employer describing his current and intended future employment.

H. *Temporary Workers and Trainees*

To qualify for a visa in this class, a prospective nonimmigrant must establish that:

1. He has a residence in a foreign country that he has no intention of abandoning.

2. He is not ineligible for a visa or excludable for any reason specified in Chapter 5, unless granted advance permission from immigration authorities to enter despite such excludability.

3. He is either:

A. Of distinguished merit and ability and coming temporarily to perform temporary services of an exceptional nature requiring such merit and ability, or

B. Coming to perform temporary services or labor if unemployed persons capable of such work cannot be found in this country, or

C. Coming temporarily as an industrial trainee.

Obviously, some contract or arrangement for employment must be made in advance before a petition to import the alien can be submitted. Otherwise an alien of distinguished merit and ability will be classified as a temporary visitor.

An "industrial trainee" is an alien coming for training either in agriculture, commerce, finance, government, transportation, or a profession. He cannot engage in productive employment if this will displace a United States resident.

PETITION BY SPONSORING EMPLOYER: No entry permit will be issued until the alien's prospective employer in the United States first files a petition with the Immigration and Naturalization Service requesting his admission to perform the services or undergo the training just described. When such a petition is approved and the consular officer so notified, the prospective entrant is eligible to apply for a visa. Notwithstanding such approval, however, the consular officer may suspend action on the visa application if he has reason to believe that the applicant is not qualified.

The petition is filed on Form I-129B at the immigration office having jurisdiction over the place where the beneficiary will work or be trained. It must be accompanied by a fee for each beneficiary, payable to the "Immigration and Naturalization Service, Department of Justice".

An employer desiring to import more than one alien may file a single petition and include all prospective employees provided all will apply for visas at the same consulate and are coming to perform the same type of service, or to receive the same type of training.

The following documents must be submitted in duplicate with the petition:

1. In the case of an alien of distinguished merit and ability:

A. A full, complete, and detailed description of higher education, technical training, specialized experience, or exceptional ability of the alien and the manner in which such qualifications were acquired.

B. Allegations of higher education must be supported by certified copies of school records showing periods of attendance, major fields of study, and degrees awarded.

C. Allegations of technical training, specialized experience, or exceptional ability must be supported by affidavits, published material, or other documents attesting to and describing the degree and extent of experience or ability, executed by the appropriate officer of the firm, organization, or other place where the alien acquired or perfected his qualifications.

2. In the case of aliens coming to perform temporary services or labor:

A. A copy of a clearance order from the United States Employment Service concerning the unavailability of like labor in the United States and showing that the policies of that agency have been observed, unless the petitioner has been informed by the Immigration and Naturalization Service that no clearance is required.

B. A statement containing a full, complete, and detailed description of the conditions making admission of the alien necessary, and showing whether the need is temporary, seasonal, or permanent, and if temporary or seasonal, whether it is expected to be recurrent.

3. In the case of an industrial trainee: a statement describing the kind of training to be given, the position or duties for which it will prepare the trainee, whether such training can be obtained outside of the United States, and explaining the need for the trainee to be trained here.

Approval of a petition is automatically terminated when the petitioner dies, goes out of business, or files a written withdrawal before arrival of the beneficiary in this country; or if a visa is not issued within one year from the date of approval of the petition.

CONDITIONS OF ADMISSION AND STAY: Upon application at the port of entry in this country, following approval of the petition and issuance of the visa, admission not in excess of one year will be authorized. A bond to insure compliance with the terms of admission may be required. When applying for admission, the worker or trainee must satisfy the immigration officer that he is destined in good faith to the employer who petitioned to import him, and that he is coming in good faith to perform the services or labor, or receive the training specified in the petition.

An extension of stay may be granted on application, in writing and under oath, by the employer or trainer. The application must contain a statement describing the alien's current and intended employment or training. If clearance from the U.S. Employment Service was required with the original petition, another clearance order must be issued, showing that the facts which justified the alien's admission continue to exist.

An employer or trainer who has imported more than one alien on the basis of a single petition may file a single application for extensions of their stay.

I. *News Reporters and Representatives of Other Information Media*

An alien applicant of this class must satisfy both consular and immigration officers that he is:

1. A bona fide representative of a foreign press, radio, film, or other information medium, who:

A. Seeks entry solely to pursue this vocation.

B. Intends in good faith, and will be able, to depart when such status ends or his period of admission expires.

C. Is not ineligible to receive a visa, as explained in Chapter 5, or

2. The spouse or child of such representative, accompanying or following to join him.

An additional precondition to the acceptability of such a representative is that his government grants similar privileges to representatives of American information media; in other words, entry permits in this category are available only on the basis of reciprocity. Hence, they will not be granted, for example, to would-be entrants from countries which bar American newsmen. This restriction applies regardless of whether the information medium involved is owned, operated, subsidized, or controlled privately or by a foreign government, with the exception of information media correspondents to the United Nations whose entry is authorized under the United Nations Headquarters Agreement irrespective of their governments' attitude toward American correspondents. However, their admission may be limited to the United Nations Headquarters area.

CONDITIONS OF ADMISSION AND STAY: Non-immigrants in this category may be admitted initially for not longer than one year or granted extensions in increments of not over one year.

J. *Exchange Visitors*

An "exchange visitor" is either an alien admitted pursuant to an "exchange-visitor program" as created by Section 201 of the United States Information and Educational Exchange Act of 1948 (as amended), or under the newly created classification of a bona fide student, scholar, trainee, teacher, professor, research assistant, or other similar specialist coming temporarily to this country to participate in a program sponsored by the Secretary of State for the pursuance of such activities.

An applicant in this class must submit a completely executed Form DSP-66 (Certificate of Eligibility for Exchange Visitor Status) issued and endorsed by his program sponsor showing the date of expiration of the participant's authorized stay as shown on his Form 1-94 (Arrival-Departure Record).

CONDITIONS OF ADMISSION AND STAY: An "exchange visitor" is admitted initially for (and granted extensions in increments of) not more than 12 months. He may not accept employment except in connection with the purpose for which he was admitted, but may transfer from one program to another. His accompanying spouse may be granted permission to accept employment, but only if necessary to support the participant and their minor children. An application for an extension of stay is also made on a current Form DSP-66.

Chapter 4

IMMIGRANTS: DOCUMENTARY AND OTHER ENTRY REQUIREMENTS

General Requirements

An immigrant generally is required to have:

1. A passport valid for at least 60 days beyond the period for which an immigrant visa is valid, for use as a document of identity and nationality and as an unconditional permit to return to the issuing country or some other foreign country, should that be necessary or required.

2. A valid unexpired visa, reentry permit, border-crossing identification card, or other entry permit. An immigrant visa is usually valid for the maximum permissible period (four months), but may be less in certain cases. In such cases, the holder may apply, without fee, for an extension up to the original allowable period of four months. If such application is made in a different consular district, the consular officer communicates with the issuing office to see if there is any objection to allowing the extension. A visa issued to a child adopted by a United States citizen (and spouse) serving abroad in the U.S. Armed Forces, or employed abroad by the U.S. Government, or temporarily abroad on business, is valid until the return of such citizen parent in due course of such service, employment, or business (but not over three years).

EXEMPTION FROM DOCUMENTARY REQUIRE-MENTS: Certain classes of immigrants are exempted either from the passport or the visa requirement. The following are not required to present *passports:*

1. A spouse, parent, unmarried son or daughter of a United States citizen or resident alien, unless coming from a country of which he or she is a national and which requires a passport for departure.
2. A resident alien returning from a temporary visit abroad (also subject to the just stated proviso).
3. A child born during a temporary visit abroad of a mother who is a resident alien or national of this country, if application for admission is made within two years after birth and the child is accompanied by his parent applying for and receiving readmission as a permanent resident on the first return to this country after said birth.
4. A stateless alien, or national of a Communist-controlled country, unable to obtain a passport, and his accompanying spouse and unmarried son or daughter.
5. A member of the United States Armed Forces.
6. A third preference immigrant (member of the profession or person of exceptional ability in the sciences or arts), and his accompanying spouse and child, unless applying for a visa in the country of which he is a national and which requires a passport for departure.
7. Any immigrant who would be exempted, except for the just stated proviso, if the Secretary of State waives the requirement.
8. An immigrant, not in an exempt category, who proves inability to obtain a passport, and for whom the Attorney General and Secretary of State waive the requirement.
9. An immigrant, satisfying the district director in charge of the port of entry that there is good cause for failure to present a passport and applying for waiver on Form 1-193.

The following are not required to obtain *visas:*

1. A child born after the issuance of a visa to his accompanying parent and applying for admission during its period of validity.
2. A child as described in item "3" of the preceding list.
3. A resident alien returning from a temporary absence abroad in any place except Albania, Cuba, Outer Mongolia, and Communist portions of China, Korea, and Vietnam, who:

   A. was absent not over one year and presents Form 1-151 (alien registration receipt card) or
   B. presents a valid unexpired reentry permit, or
   C. is the spouse or child of, and resided abroad with, a member of the United States Armed Forces, stationed abroad under official orders, or
   D. satisfies the district director at the port of entry that there is good cause for failure to present a visa, and applies for waiver on Form 1-193.

A Form 1-151 alien registration receipt card is invalid for reentry of an alien who, during a temporary stay abroad, was at any time in Albania, Cuba, Outer Mongolia or Communist portions of China, Korea or Vietnam or—except for a child under 16 when applying for admission—Bulgaria, Estonia, Hungary, Latvia, Lithuania, Poland, Romania, East Germany, Yugoslavia, or the Soviet Union, unless such alien passed in direct, restricted, and continuous transit through East Germany to Berlin from West Germany by auto, rail, or plane and returned to West Germany, or through Yugoslavia to or from Austria, Italy or Greece. An immigrant visa, reentry permit, or Form 1-151 is also invalid if such alien would be entitled to non-immigrant status as a foreign government official, treaty trader or investor, or foreign government representative to an international organization, unless he has previously submitted, or submits, an application for admission, or written waiver of the right to adjustment of status.

4. A member of the United States Armed Forces in uniform or bearing identifying documents, previously admitted for permanent residence, and proceeding to the United States under official orders or permit.
5. A resident alien entering the continental United States, or any place under United Statess jurisdiction, directly from Guam, Puerto Rico, or the Virgin Islands.
6. An American Indian born in Canada, having at least 50% blood of the American Indian race.

Procedure for Obtaining an Immigrant Visa

Application for an Immigration visa is made on Form FS-510 at the consular office having jurisdiction over the prospective immigrant's place of residence. However, an application by an alien physically present in another consular district may, in the discretion of the consular officer or State Department, be accepted. Separate applications must be submitted for each alien applying for a visa, but a child under 14 years of age, or a physically handicapped person, may have his application executed on his behalf by his parent or guardian, or, if there is no parent or guardian, any person having legal custody of, or a legitimate interest in him. Every applicant must appear personally before the consular officer, although this requirement may, in the latter's discretion, be waived for an applicant under 14 years of age. Any applicant may, in the consular officer's discretion, be required to complete Form FS-497 (Preliminary Questionnaire to Determine Immigrant Status) in order to assist the consular officer in his determination of the applicant's classification and chargeability.

Every pertinent question on the form must be answered and every blank space filled out with the information called for, after which the application must be signed and sworn to before the consular officer. A fee is collected and payment indicated by a fee stamp pasted to the application and cancelled by the consular officer. An additional fee is charged for issuance of the visa. Such fees are returnable only when the officer in charge of the consulate or issuing post finds that a visa was erroneously issued or is unusable because of government action for which the alien was not responsible.

INFORMATION REQUIRED: The application must state the full and true name of the applicant and any other he has ever used or been known by; his age and sex; date and place of birth; present address and places of previous residence; marital status and names and residence of his spouse and children, if any; occupation; personal description; languages he can speak, read, or write; names and addresses of parents, or, if neither parent is living, of his next of kin in the country from which he comes; port of entry to the United States and destination beyond, if any; whether he has a ticket to such final destination; whether he is coming to join a relative or friend, and, if so, the latter's name and address; the purpose and length of his intended stay; whether he was ever arrested, convicted, or placed in a prison or almshouse, or has been the beneficiary of a pardon or amnesty; whether he was ever treated in an institution, hospital, or other place for insanity or mental disease; if claiming "immediate relative," "special immigrant," or preference immigrant status, the facts on which the claim is based; whether he is a member of a class excluded under the immigration laws, or claiming exemption from such exclusion; and any other information required by the consular officer.

SUPPORTING DOCUMENTS: The following documentation, if obtainable, must accompany the application:

1. *Police Certificate*
Two certified copies stating what such records show concerning the applicant, including any and all arrests, the reasons therefor, and disposition of each case of which there is a record.

2. *Prison Record*
Two certified copies containing a report of the applicant's confinement in a penal or corrective institution, including a report of his conduct while confined.

3. *Military Record*
Two certified copies containing a record of applicant's service and conduct while in such service, including any convictions for crimes before military tribunals (a certificate of discharge from the military forces or an enrollment book is not acceptable in place of an official military record, unless showing the applicant's complete service record; however, the consular officer may wish to see the discharge certificate or enrollment book even though incomplete).

4. *Birth Certificate*
A birth certificate or other birth record showing the date and place of birth, and the parentage of the applicant, issued by the official custodian of such records in the country of birth, and based on the official registration thereof. An alien who has only one such certificate and cannot obtain another may present two certified or photostatic copies, but the original must be exhibited to the consular officer, who may then return it.

5. *Photographs*

Three photographs, one unsigned and two signed (so as not to obscure the features), reflecting a reasonable likeness of the applicant at the time presented; one and one-half inches square; unmounted; printed on a light background and showing a full front view of the face, without head covering.

6. *Other Documents*

Any other documents or records required by the consular officer. This refers to any official records which may help that official to determine the applicant's identity, proper classification, and eligibility to receive an immigrant visa.

If satisfied that a document or record is unobtainable, the consular officer may accept any other satisfactory evidence. A document is considered unobtainable if it cannot be procured without actual hardship other than normal inconvenience and delay. If a consular officer has any reason to believe that a document or record is not authentic or has been tampered with, he may take whatever action he deems necessary.

REFUSAL OF APPLICATION: A visa application will be considered defective and will not be approved if:

1. The applicant fails to furnish any information called for in the application or by the consular officer.

2. The application is not supported by the necessary documents.

3. The applicant refuses to be fingerprinted.

4. The necessary fees are not paid either for the application or the visa.

5. The applicant fails to swear to or affirm the application before the consular officer, or

6. The application fails in some other respect to meet

the legal requirements for reasons for which the applicant is responsible.

REFUSAL OF VISA: If advised that a visa cannot be issued, the applicant may prefer not to file a formal application and thus save the fee. There can be no formal refusal unless an application is executed. When a visa application is refused, Form FS-510 and supporting documents are returned to the applicant, and copies kept in the consulate files. If the asserted ground of ineligibility can be overcome by the presentation of additional evidence submitted within 120 days, the consular officer will retain the application and documents for such period, awaiting such evidence, and if the same is submitted, will reconsider the application without payment of an additional fee.

REVOCATION OF VISA: A visa may be revoked if the consular officer finds that it was procured by deceit or concealment, or that the alien was, or has become, ineligible. Where practicable, notice of proposed revocation is given the alien and opportunity to show cause why it should not be made. Notice also is given to the transportation line and a report sent to the Secretary of State for transmission to the Attorney General. If the visa is revoked, the alien is also requested to surrender it to the consular officer, who will write the word "Revoked" across its face, and sign and date the notation. Any legend in the passport concerning the issuance of the visa will also be cancelled. Documents furnished by the alien may or may not be returned, in the consular officer's discretion. He must, however, consider any evidence submitted by the alien, his attorney, or representative, indicating that revocation was improper, and if he so decides, a new visa or replacement will be issued.

REVALIDATION, REPLACEMENT, AND TRANS-
FER OF VISA: As noted at the outset of the chapter, a
visa issued for less than the maximum permissible period
of four months may be extended to encompass that
period, and without an additional fee. Application may
be made at any consular office, but, if other than the
issuing office, such office is contacted to ascertain if any
reason exists for denial of the request.

If an "immediate relative" or "special immigrant" visa
is lost, mutilated, or expires, a new one may be issued at
any consular office upon payment of full fees for
application and visa, provided, of course, the immigrant
remains qualified. Where a preference or nonpreference
visa is lost, mutilated, or unusable for reasons beyond the
control of the holder, and for which he is not responsible,
a replacement under the same number, for the same year,
may be issued on full payment of fees, provided the
immigrant remains eligible, and the consular officer is in
possession of a duplicate signed consular or receiving
office file copy of the original.

The case of a visa applicant, pending in one consular
office, may be transferred to another consular office at
the request—and risk—of the applicant, if there is
reasonable justification for such action, and the transferring office has no reason to believe that the applicant will
be unable to appear at the receiving office to apply. In an
appropriate case, such a transfer may include authorization to grant "immediate relative" or preference immigrant
status upon an approved petition. However, visa *numbers*
may not be transferred and must be returned immediately
to the State Department.

*"Special Immigrants," "Immediate Relatives" and Prefer-
ence Immigrants*

In addition to the general visa requirements already
outlined, there are certain other prerequisites in the case

of "immediate relatives," "special" and "preference immigrants." In this connection, it is important to note
certain statutory definitions, and also to bear in mind
that where a spouse and child of a privileged immigrant
claim the same exemption or priority only on the basis of
the latter's eligibility and receipt of a visa, in order for
them to be admitted with such classification, the principal
immigrant must have been actually permitted to enter
this country so classified. A "spouse" does not include a
person claiming such status by reason of a marriage
ceremony where the parties were not physically in each
other's presence, as in a proxy or picture marriage, unless
the marriage is consummated. With this exception,
however, the terms "husband" or "wife" do denote a
"spouse," if the marriage is recognized as valid under the
laws of the country where it took place. A "child" is an
unmarried person under 21 years of age. The term
includes an "illegitimate" child for whom a status,
privilege, or benefit is sought by reason of its relationship
to its natural mother. It does not include a stepchild,
unless he was under 18 years of age when the marriage
making him such occurred, nor an adopted child, unless
adopted while under the age of 14, and thereafter in the
legal custody of, and residing with, the adopting parents
for at least two years. Conversely, these same conditions
determine whether or not an "adoptive" or stepparent is a
"parent" within the meaning of the immigration laws.

PROOF OF FINANCIAL STATUS: The consular
officer must be satisfied that the visa applicant is not
likely to become a public charge. If he is without
adequate funds or assurance of employment, he may be
required to furnish affidavits of support by persons in the
United States (usually two) guaranteeing that he will not
have to rely upon public assistance. Where petitions are
filed on behalf of "immediate relatives," "special im-

migrants" and preference immigrants by relatives in the United States, they may not only be required to submit affidavits of support, but also proof of financial ability to furnish the same, such as:

1. A statement of an employer, preferably on his business stationery, showing date and nature of employment, salary paid, and whether the position is temporary or permanent.

2. If self-employed, a copy of his last income tax return, or report of a commercial rating concern.

3. A statement from the bank or other financial institution in which he maintains his deposits, showing the date the account was opened, total deposits for the past year, and present balance.

4. A list or statement showing serial number and denominations of bonds and name of purchaser.

5. Additional affidavits of support from near relatives.

No time limitation is placed upon the obligation to support. However, the practice of requiring such affidavits is not derived from any statute or regulation, and it has been held that a sponsor cannot be held responsible if the beneficiary becomes a public charge.

INFORMAL EXAMINATION: If a visa applicant proposes to precede his family to this country, the consular officer may arrange an examination of other members of the family to determine whether there then exists any mental, physical, or other ineligibility to receive an immigrant visa. If so, the applicant is informed and required to acknowledge such notification in writing. However, the fact that he is not so informed is no assurance that visas will be issued to his family. Their eligibility for visas is determined only upon making formal application, and their admissibility is again subject to scrutiny when they reach the port of entry.

PHYSICAL AND MENTAL EXAMINATION: Every applicant must submit to such a check-up to help the consular officer determine his eligibility for a visa. Where U.S Public Health Service medical officers are available, the examination is conducted by them; otherwise, by a reputable and competent doctor selected by the applicant from an approved panel of physicians. If laboratory facilities are not available for the necessary tests, the tests are made at the port of entry in the United States, and the alien may, of course, be excluded on findings then made. A fee is charged if the examination is conducted by physicians of the U.S. Public Health Service, except in the cases of aliens entering under government sponsored programs, and refugees.

REGISTRATION AND FINGERPRINTING: Every applicant for an immigrant visa must be registered (which occurs automatically when the executed application is submitted), and, unless a child under 14 years of age, fingerprinted.

ISSUANCE OF VISA: If the application is approved, approval is recorded on Form FS-511 (Immigrant Visa and Alien Registration), with a notation indicated that a petition (if one was used) is attached, date of issuance and expiration, the immigrant's classification, and symbols and number indicating the foreign state or subquota to which he is chargeable. If the principal consular officer considers it desirable to number "immediate relative" and "special immigrant" visas, they must be numbered consecutively, beginning a new series every July 1. If a passport has been waived, a notation is made in the space provided for the passport number setting forth the authority (section and paragraph) under which it was waived. The form is signed by the consular officer, and the alien's photograph is attached in the space provided, by use of a legend machine unless specific authorization has been granted by the State Department to use the impression seal only. The "visa" consists of Form FS-510, Form FS-511, and a copy of each required document.

SPECIAL IMMIGRANTS: As already noted, a "special immigrant" (or an "immediate relative") is admissible without numerical restriction. As between the several classes of "special immigrants," there is no priority. However, consular officers are authorized to establish waiting lists where the demand for visas is so heavy that all applications cannot be acted on concurrently from day to day. The purpose of this procedure is simply to establish an orderly schedule of appointments under a system of advance examination of the documents of prospective immigrants. The elements of eligibility and procedure vary according to the individual category of "special immigrant" involved, and it is well, therefore, to consider each class separately.

1. *Natives of Independent Countries of the Western Hemisphere and the Canal Zone*

Eligibility for entry under this classification extends to spouses and children of the principal aliens, if accompanying or following to join them, or if the marriage or birth creating such relationship occurred after entry of the principal alien. The newly independent countries of Jamaica, Trinidad-Tobago, Barbados, and Guyana, formerly charged to British subquotas, are now included in the defined area. The exemption from numerical restrictions on entry of this subclass will end on June 30, 1968, after which there will be an annual ceiling of 120,000 (exclusive of entrants who are also "immediate relatives" and entering as such). (The term "native" refers to the place of birth and nothing else).

2. *Returning Resident Aliens*

Any alien previously admitted for permanent residence,

who is returning from a temporary visit abroad, is eligible for a "special immigrant" visa unless otherwise excludable under the immigration laws as explained in Chapter 7. The elements of eligibility which he must establish are:

A. That he had the status of an alien lawfully admitted for permanent residence at the time he left the United States; if the consul has reason to question this, he may require verificaton from the Immigration and Naturalization Service at the expense of the alien.

B. That he departed from this country with the intention of returning.

C. That he is returning to this country from a temporary visit abroad. If his stay abroad was protracted, he must show that it was because of reasons beyond his control and for which he was not responsible.

A returning resident alien may be required to furnish the same documents usually presented by other immigrants with their visa applications if the consul considers this necessary. He may also be asked to exhibit his alien registration receipt card and any unexpired reentry permit that may have been issued to him. Of course, if he has a valid reentry permit (or alien registration receipt card—and has been abroad not more than one year) he need not present a passport or visa in applying at the port of entry, although he is, of course, subject to exclusion on other grounds, as explained in Chapter 5. A resident alien contemplating a trip abroad may, therefore, prefer to procure a reentry permit before departure, especially if expecting to be away for more than a year. As already noted, use of the alien registration receipt card for reentry is restricted to residents absent for not more than one year. While the initial period of validity of a reentry permit is similarly limited, the permit may be extended.

PROCEDURE FOR OBTAINING REENTRY PERMIT: Any alien lawfully admitted for permanent residence, and physically present in the United States, may apply to any local office of the Immigration and Naturalization Service, on Form 1-131, for a reentry permit. The application must be submitted at least 30 days prior to departure, accompanied by the applicant's alien registration receipt card (Form 1-151) (unless the latter is in the process of being issued). A separate application is required of each alien applying, regardless of age or sex. A parent or guardian may execute an application on behalf of a child under 14 years of age. A fee must accompany the application.

If the applicant is engaged in an occupation which would entitle him to diplomatic, "international organization," or "treaty trader" classification, he must execute a waiver of immunities (on Form 1-508), unless he has already done so. If the local immigration office finds that he is qualified and applying in good faith, and that his departure will not be prejudicial to the interests of the United States, a reentry permit (Form 1-132) will be issued (for use during a period not to exceed one year—although it may be less in some instances).

If the applicatin is denied, the applicant may, within 15 days of the mailing of notice thereof, appeal to the regional commissioner, whose decision is final. If the denial is upheld, the fee is returned.

If an applicant finds that it is absolutely necessary to leave the United States before securing the permit, and satisfies the immigration authorities that it is a bona fide emergency, arrangements will be made to forward the permit to a consular officer abroad for delivery. However, an officer of the Immigration and Naturalization Service should be consulted before the applicant leaves the country.

No reentry permit, or extension, will be granted to any alien subject to registration for service in the U.S. Armed Forces unless he first obtains the consent of his local draft board to leave the country. The validity of the permit will then depend upon the period of absence allowed by the draft board, but in no event to exceed one year.

If the holder of the permit desires an extension, he must file an application prior to the expiration date at the immigration office in the district of his residence or foreign office having juridiction of his place of temporary sojourn. It may be filed with an American consular officer if the applicant is temporarily in one of the following places: South America (exept Venezuela); Asia-east of the western borders of Afghanistan and Pakistan (except Hong Kong and adjacent islands, Taiwan, Japan, Okinawa, Korea, and the Philippines); Australia, New Zealand, Bulgaria, Czechslovakia, Hungary, Iceland, Romania, Soviet Union, Iran, Iraq, Jordan, Saudi Arabia, Syrian Arab Republic, Yemen, Aden, Kuwait; and Africa (including the United Arab Republic). While filing prior to expiration of the permit is prescribed, this requirement is fulfilled by timely mailing of the application though it be received after the date of expiration.

Application for extension is filed on Form 1-143, accompanied by a fee, and must state the reasons for requesting an extension and the address to which it is to be mailed. Remittances should be made payable to the "Immigration and Naturalization Service, Department of Justice." The original permit must also accompany the application. An approval is noted on the permit which is returned in person or by mail if the applicant is in this country, and, if abroad, through the nearest consular officer or directly to the address specified in the application. If the application be denied, the permit is returned only if its period of validity has not expired. During this period, a permit may be used for any number of reentries. Extensions may be granted for periods not in the aggregate exceeding one year from the original date of expiration. If an alien leaves without a reentry permit, or has a permit which expires while he is abroad, he must apply to a consular officer for a "special immigrant" visa, or to an immigration officer for waiver of a visa.

PROCEDURE FOR OBTAINING AN ALIEN REGISTRATION RECEIPT CARD: Application for this document (Form 1-151) is submitted on Form 1-90, accompanied by two photographs and a fee. The card is available to aliens previously admitted for permanant residence, and is valid indefinitely for use in place of a "special immigrant" visa or reentry permit following visits abroad of not over one year.

3. *Certain Former Citizens*
This class consists of two groups:

A. Women Expatriates
A "woman expatriate" is a former United States citizen who lost her citizenship through marriage to an alien or by loss of he husband's citizenship prior to September 22, 1922, or, on or after that date, by marriage to an alien ineligible for citizenship, and who has not acquired another nationality by any affirmative act other than marriage (e.g., by accepting foreign citizenship or taking an oath of allegiance to a foreign state).

Between March 2, 1907 and September 22, 1922, the law provided that a female citizen who married an alien took his citizenship and lost her own. Moreover, marriage to a person of Asiatic blood, ineligible for citizenship under the law then in effect, also resulted in loss of the citizenship (this provision was effective until March 3, 1931).

Persons suffering expatriation in this manner, however, were permitted to reacquire their nationality in various ways. While women who became citizens by birth may, if abroad, reacquire citizenship by taking the oath of allegiance before a U.S. consular or diplomatic officer, those who originally acquired citizenship in any other manner must return and be naturalized if they took up or maintained a foreign residence following their marriage.

The naturalization laws require that a person in the latter category be lawfully admitted for permanent residence. A woman expatriate in this class, seeking reentry for the purpose of repatriation, is eligible for a "special immigrant" visa without quota restriction or delay, and such eligibility is unaffected by her immediate marital status. A native-born woman expatriate who prefers to take the oath of repatriation before a naturalization court instead of a consular or diplomatic officer abroad is also eligible for a "special immigrant" visa.

B. Military Expatriates

A "military expatriate" is a former United States citizen who lost his citizenship by entering or serving in the armed forces of a foreign state between September 1, 1939 and September 2, 1945, provided:

1. Such country was allied with the United States between December 7, 1941 and September 2, 1945; and

2. Such country was not at war with the United States during any period of his military service.

A prospective immigrant is also entitled to such status if he lost citizenship by:

1. Entering the military, naval, or air forces of an allied country, whether or not he performed any military service; or

2. Taking an oath of allegiance in order to enter the military service of an allied country, whether or not he served.

Prior to January 13, 1941 no person could lose American citizenship through military service unless he voluntarily took an oath of allegiance in connection with such service. From that date until December 23, 1952, military service alone was sufficient to cause loss of citizenship if the participant had or acquired the nationality of the country in whose forces he served.

4. *Ministers of Religion*

To qualify for this status, an applicant must satisfy the consular officer that he is a minister of a religious denomination having a bona fide organization in the United States requiring his services, and that, for at least two years immediately before applying he has been engaged continuously, and seeks entry solely for the purpose of engaging in such calling. The sponsoring organization must first file a petition with the immigration service to so classify the applicant, and it must be approved and forwarded to the consular officer before he may entertain the application for a "special immigrant" visa. Upon fulfillment of all these requirements, visas will be issued to the applicant, and his spouse and children (if any) who are accompanying or following to join him. As noted earlier, the term "minister" denotes a person duly authorized to conduct religious worship and other functions regularly conducted by regularly ordained pastors of the denomination involved, and no other.

PROCEDURE FOR FILING PETITION ON BEHALF OF A MINISTER: This petition is submitted by the sponsoring organization for which the services are to be performed (on Form 1-130) to the immigration office having jurisdiction over the place where the beneficiary will be employed. It must be accompanied by a statement, preferably on official stationery, respecting the ordination or other authorization of the beneficiary to act as a minister, and setting forth the name of each religious sect or denomination served, periods of service, and addresses where such services were performed during the preceding two years. Such statement must be signed by the appropriate official having knowledge of the beneficiary's religious service abroad and show the source of such knowledge. The petition must be sworn to before a notary public or other officer authorized to administer oaths (if executed outside the United States, the oath may be taken before a consular officer). A fee for each beneficiary, payable to the "Immigration and Naturalization Service, Department of Justice," must be remitted.

If satisfied that the beneficiary is eligible for "special immigrant" status, the immigration office will approve the petition. If, however, it appears that he is ineligible for any reason, the sponsor will be advised and may withdraw its petition. The fee, however, will not be returned. If a petition is disapproved, the petitioner may appeal within 10 days after notice thereof, to the Central Office of the Immigration and Naturalization Service, where a final decision will be made.

An approved petition is valid for one year from the date of approval and for such additional periods as extended by the immigration authorities. An approved petition will be automatically revoked, however, if:

1. The beneficiary is not issued a visa within one year of the date of approval of the petition; or

2. The petitioner dies, goes out of business, or files a written withdrawal of the petition before arrival of the beneficiary in this country to apply for admission.

5. *Employees of U.S. Government Abroad*

An alien may be granted a "special immigrant" visa if:

A. He has served faithfully for at least 15 years as an employee of one or more agencies of the United States

Government abroad (not necessarily including the Foreign Service).

B. The principal officer of a Foreign Service establishment has recommended such classification of the visa applicant under exceptional circumstances, and the Secretary of State approves the recommendation and finds the granting of such status to be in the national interest.

If these conditions exist, "special immigrant" status and visas may also be granted to his accompanying spouse and children.

PREFERENCE IMMIGRANTS AND IMMEDIATE RELATIVES: Before a visa may be issued to a preference immigrant or "immediate relative" a petition to be so classified must be filed and approved. The procedure varies according to the status claimed. In some categories, the petition is made by the applicant; in some, by the sponsor, and in still others, by either. Certification by the Secretary of Labor of the non-availability of like labor in this country and in the locality of intended employment, and that such employment will not adversely affect wages and working conditions of similarly employed workers in this country is required in the case of:

1. All nonpreference immigrants.

2. Third preference and sixth preference immigrants (members of the professions and persons with exceptional ability in the sciences or arts; and skilled and unskilled workers).

3. "Special immigrants" who are natives of independent countries of the Western Hemisphere or Canal Zone (other than parents, spouses, or children of U.S. citizens or resident aliens).

Such certification is not required of other immigrants, i.e., those in the "relative" preference categories, "immediate relatives," and refugees; nor is it required of elderly applicants and others who can prove that they will not seek employment in the United States.

Aliens requiring certification apply a Form ES-575 (available at consular offices, or immigration offices (for those applying for adjustment of status)). This form consists of two parts: Part A, which is filed out by the alien ("Qualifications of Alien"), and Part B, which is filled out by the employer ("Job Offer for Alien Employment"). The employer then submits the completed form (ES-575-A and ES-575B) to the local State Employment Service office, and later attaches the certification (if issued) to this petition on behalf of the prospective employee. Third preference immigrants (members of professions or persons with exceptional ability in the sciences or arts) *may* fill out their own forms (just Part A) and forward it, together with their petitions and evidence of qualifications to the Bureau of Employment Security, Department of Labor.

Blanket Certification

The Department of Labor has issued a blanket certification for certain specified categories of employment in which applicants, accordingly, need no individual certifications. The list currently in effect covers the following:

1. Persons who received an advanced degree in a particular field of study from an institution of higher learning accredited in the country where the degree was obtained (comparable to a Ph.D., or master's degree given in American colleges or universities).

2. Persons who received a degree conferred by an accredited institution of higher learning, or have experience or a combination of experience and education equivalent to such a degree in:

Accounting and Auditing.

Aeronautical Engineering.

Architecture.
Chemical Engineering.
Chemistry.
Civil Engineering.
Dietetics.
Electrical Engineering.
Electronic Engineering.
Industrial Engineering.
Mathematics.
Mathematical Engineering.
Metallurgy and Metallurgical Engineering.
Nuclear Engineering.
Nursing.
Pharmacy.
Physical Therapy.
Physics

3. Certain persons coming to conduct religious services or engage in specified religious activities (the specific requirements and conditions are quite detailed).

Excluded Occupations

The Department of Labor has also published a list of occupations for which certification will not currently be issued, either because of the availability of sufficient workers in this country, or because alien employment therein would adversely affect working conditions of similarly employed workers here. For the most part, these are occupations where shortages are quickly filled by resident workers. The list is obtainable at immigration, consular, and state employment service offices. Applicants in these categories are informed that there is practically no chance of obtaining certification, but they may, nevertheless, sent their applications to would-be employers for completion and submission to the local state employment service office. In exceptional cases, where it is possible to show that there is a need in a particular area and such employment will not adversely affect working conditions in this country, certifications may issue.

PROCEDURE FOR SUBMITTING PETITIONS: Regulations governing the submission of petitions vary with the respective categories and will be considered under the appropriate headings.

1. *Petition for Classification as "Immediate Relative" or Preference Immigrant in the "Relative" Categories (other than petition for an orphan)*

This petition is submitted on Form 1-130, accompanied by Form G-325 (Biographic Information) executed by petitioner and a separate such form executed by petitioner's spouse, to the immigration office having jurisdiction over petitioner's place of residence, and if this be outside of the United States to the foreign immigration service office designated to act thereon. This can be determined by consulting the nearest American consul. It may be submitted to consular officers in certain designated areas if petitioner and beneficiary are both present, but any petition not clearly approvable must be referred to the appropriate immigration service office. The areas where consular offices may act are:

1. Visa-issuing posts in South America (excluding Venezuela).

2. Areas of Asia east of the western borders of Afghanistan and Pakistan (excluding Hong Kong and adjacent islands, Taiwan, Japan, Okinawa, Korea, and the Philippines).

3. Australia, New Zealand, and Africa (excluding the United Arab Republic, Mediterranean islands, and Portuguese island possessions).

Notification of decision is mailed to the petitioner, including, in case of denial, the reasons therefor, and the right of appeal, within 15 days of such mailing, to the Board of Immigration Appeals.

2. *Petition on Behalf of Orphan*

This petition is submitted on Form 1-600, accompanied by Form G-325 (Biographic Information) executed by petitioner and a separate such form executed by petitioner's spouse, to the immigration office having jurisdiction over petitioner's place of residence, and if this be outside of the United States, to the designated foreign office of the immigration service. If intending to go abroad to adopt an orphan, petitioner may submit a request to the district director of the immigration office to begin preliminary processing of the case before filing of the petition. After the petition is submitted and considered, petitioner is notified of the decision, and, if adverse, of the reasons and his right to appeal to the regional commissioner.

3. *Petition for Third Preference Immigrant*

A petition to classify an alien as a third preference immigrant (member of the professions or person of exceptional ability in the sciences or arts) is submitted on Form 1-140, either by the alien or any person on his behalf, to the immigration office having jurisdiction over the petitioner's place or residence and accompanied by Form ES-575-A (Qualifications of Alien). An alien abroad, petitioning in his own behalf, executes the oath or affirmation before an immigration or consular officer, who supplies the address of the immigration office in this country to which the petition must be sent. Petitioners may, as a matter of discretion, be required to appear for interrogation under oath by a consular or immigration officer respecting the allegations of the petition before action thereon. Notice of decision is given to the petitioner and, if adverse, the reasons and his right to appeal to the regional commissioner.

4. *Petition for Sixth Preference Immigrant*

A petition for such classification (skilled or unskilled worker) is submitted by the prospective employer on Form 1-140 (executed under oath), together with a labor certification, to the immigration office having jurisdiction over the place where the work is to be done. Petitioners may be required, as a matter of discretion, to appear for questioning under oath regarding the allegations in the petition; are notified of the decision and, in case of denial, the reasons and right of appeal to the regional commissioner.

5. *Application for Conditional Entry*

Application for conditional entry of a refugee is filed on Form 1-590 with the officer in charge of the nearest immigration office outside of the United States, together with Form 1-591 (assurance of employment and housing in the United States for two years.) Notice of decision is given but no appeal lies from a denial.

6. *Documentary Requirements*

If the beneficiary is in the United States, his passport and Form 1-94 (Arrival-Departure Record) (if issued) must be submitted with the petition. Proof of citizenship must be submitted by one claiming such status and petitioning for a relative or orphan. If a citizen by birth, he must present a birth certificate, or if this be unobtainable, a copy of his baptismal record (if this be unobtainable, he may present affidavits of two U.S. citizens with personal knowledge of his birth in this country; if petitioning outside of the United States, proof of birth may be established by a valid unexpired passport showing the date and place of birth, or, in lieu thereof, a statement from a consular officer certifying the petitioner to be a citizen and bearer of such a passport). A native-born citizen serving in the Armed Forces outside of the country and submitting a petition without the usual proof of birth may submit a statement by an appropriate officer of the Armed Forces that the service personnel records show that he was born in the United States on a certain date, provided such officer finds that requiring the usual documentary proof would cause the petitioner unusual delay and hardship. A petitioning citizen, naturalized prior to September 27, 1906 or within 90 days preceding the filing of the petition, must submit his naturalization certificate with the petition. A citizen by reason of the citizenship of a parent or husband must present evidence of the citizenship and marriage of the parent or husband, and of the legal termination of all previous marriages. If claiming citizenship through a parent, the petitioner must also present his birth certificate and a statement of the date, port, and means of all his arrivals and departures into and out of the country. If the petitioner claims lawful admission as a permanent resident alien, this must be verified by the official immigration service records, or in the absence of such proof, by evidence such as a passport bearing a Service endorsement showing such admission for permanent residence, Form 1-151 (Alien Registration Receipt Card) or an immigrant identification card.

EVIDENCE OF FAMILY RELATIONSHIP: A petition for classification of an alien as an "immediate relative," or preference immigrant in one of the "relative" categories, must be accompanied by evidence of the claimed family relationship. The following evidentiary requirements are prescribed:

1. *Petition for Spouse*
A marriage certificate and proof of the legal termination of all prior marriages of both spouses.

2. *Petition for Child*

If the petition is submitted by the mother, regardless of the child's age, its birth certificate showing the mother's name. If submitted by the father or stepparent, regardless of the child's age, a certificate of the parents' marriage, legal termination of all prior marriages of both, and the child's birth certificate.

3. *Petition for a Brother or Sister*

Birth certificate of petitioner and beneficiary, showing a common mother. If there be a common father, but different mothers, marriage certificates of petitioner's and beneficiary's parents, and proof of legal termination of all prior marriages.

4. *Petition for Parent*
  A. Petition for Mother:
    Petitioner's birth certificate showing mother's name.
  B. Petition for Father or Stepparent:
    Petitioner's birth certificate, marriage certificate of parent and stepparent, and proof of legal termination of all prior marriages.

5. *Married Women*

If either petitioner or beneficiary is a married woman, her marriage certificate, but if the relationship is that of mother and child, the mother's marriage certificate is unnecessary if her present name appears on the child's birth certificate.

6. *Relationship by Adoption*
    Certified copy of adoption decree.

7. *Petition for Orphan*

A. Evidence of United States citizenship of petitioning husband and wife.

B. Marriage certificate of petitioner and spouse, and proof of legal termination of all prior marriages.

C. Proof of orphan's age by birth certificate if available; otherwise, by other proof.

D. Evidence that petitioner and spouse can care for orphan properly, such as letters from employers, banks and accountants, financial statements, income tax returns, etc.

E. Certified copy of adoption decree (with certified translation if orphan adopted abroad).

F. Evidence that sole or surviving parent is incapable of providing for the orphan's care, and has in writing irrevocably released the orphan for emigration and adoption, if the orphan has only one parent.

G. Fingerprint charts of petitioning husband and spouse (on Form DR-258)

H. Evidence of compliance with preadoption requirements:

(1) If adoption is to take place in the United States, evidence of compliance with preadoption requirements of state of proposed residence, except such requirements as cannot be satisfied before arrival in this country.

(2) If adoption took place abroad, without the orphan having been seen and observed by petitioner and wife before or during the adoption proceedings, the adoptive parents must submit a statement of intent to readopt in this country, unless the immigration authorities have determined from the state of proposed residence (by statement from adoption Court, Department of Welfare, or State Attorney General) that such readoption is permissible, and evidence of compliance with preadoption requirements. In such cases, the orphan is processed as a child to be adopted in the United States.

EVIDENCE OF QUALIFICATION: Documentary evidence of qualification is required in support of third and sixth preference petitions. As these vary with the category, they will be considered separately.

1. *Petition for Third Preference Classification*

A petition to classify an alien as a member of the professions or person of exceptional ability in the sciences or arts must be accompanied by Form ES-575A (Qualifications of Alien) unless the profession or specialty is included in the blanket certification list, and evidence of qualification, unless the alien is clearly qualified or clearly not within the purview of the statute. These documents, when required, are forwarded to the Bureau of Employment Security, Department of Labor, which, after review, notifies the immigration service as to the issuance of certification. If qualification is based, wholly or partly, on high education, the petition must be accompanied by a certified copy of the alien's school record (showing period of attendance, major study, and degrees awarded). Any license or permit to practice must also be submitted. If qualfication is based on exceptional ability in the sciences or arts, documentary evidence such as affidavits by past or present employers, or recognized experts familiar with the alien's work or published material must be presented, showing how affiants acquired their knowledge of such qualification, the dates and places of the alien's acquisition of exceptional ability, and detailed description of duties performed by him. Published material (by or about the alien) must be accompanied by dates and titles.

2. *Petition for Sixth Preference Classification*

An applicant for a sixth preference visa (skilled or unskilled labor) receives Form ES-575 from the consular officer, completes Part A (Qualifications of Alien), and sends the form to his prospective employer, who completes, Part B (Job Offer for Alien Employment) and submits the fully executed form to the local State Employment Service office. If certification is issued to the employer, it is endorsed on Form ES-575A, together with the Department of Labor's advisory opinion concerning the beneficiary's qualifications, and the employer files the certification and supporting documentary evidence with his petition. If the beneficiary's qualifications are based, wholly or partly, on higher education or attendance at a technical or vocational school, this must be evidenced by a certified copy of his school record (showing period of attendance, major study, and degrees). If based on technical training, specialized experience, or exceptional ability, the claim of qualification must be supported by documentary evidence such as affidavits or published material.

Period of Validity of Approved Petition

An approved petition for a third or sixth preference immigrant is valid for one year from the date of labor certification, or, in the case of blanket certification, from the date of the petition's approval. An approved "immediate relative" or preference class relative petition is valid for five years from the date of approval.

Conversion of Classification

A valid petition classifying a child of a citizen as an "immediate relative" or unmarried son or daughter of a citizen (first preference immigrant) automatically converts to approved status as a fourth preference immigrant (married son or daughter of citizen) as of the date the beneficiary marries, whereas the latter status converts to first preference status, upon giving satisfactory evidence of the legal termination of the beneficiary's marriage, or, if the beneficiary is under 21 at the date of such termination, to "immediate relative" status. A child who is an "immediate relative" automatically becomes a first preference immigrant upon reaching the age of 21. A spouse, unmarried son or daughter of a resident alien (second preference category) if under the age of 21 becomes an "immediate relative" upon naturalization of said alien; if over 21, the son or daughter becomes a first preference immigrant.

Revocation of Approved Petition

1. *Automatic Revocation*
Approval of a petition is automatically revoked by any of the following events:

A. *"Relative" Petitions*
(1) Formal withdrawal by the petitioner.
(2) Death of petitioner or beneficiary.
(3) Legal termination of husband-wife relationship (first or second preference categories).
(4) Attainment of age of 21 by child who was "immediate relative," except as valid for five years to accord first preference status, if remaining unmarried and fourth preference status in the event of marriage.
(5) Marriage of first preference immigrant, except as valid for five years to accord fourth preference status.
(6) Marriage of son or daughter (second preference category).
(7) Nonissuance of visa on or before expiration date of approved petition's validity (third and sixth preference categories).
(8) Death or termination of business of petitioner (third and sixth preference categories).

(9) Cancellation, withdrawal, or expiration of labor certification (third and sixth preference categories).

(10) Expiration of period of validity of petition or last revalidation.

2. *Revocation on Notice*

On notice to petitioner, and opportunity to offer opposing evidence, an immigration officer, authorized to approve petitions, may revoke an approval when the propriety thereof is brought to the attention of the immigration service, including requests for reconsideration or revocation made by consular officers. Notice of revocation is mailed to petitioner, including the reasons therefor and the right of appeal within 15 days of such mailing.

Revalidation

An *automatically* revoked petition may be revalidated retroactively, as of the date of application therefor, if current eligibility exists. The petitioner applies to the district director (consular officers in specified areas) who may revalidate a petition when petitioner and beneficiary are both present, but must refer any not clearly subject to revalidation to the appropriate immigration officer outside of the United States. Petitioner is notified of the decision, and, if adverse, the reasons and of his right to appeal within 15 days of the mailing of such notification, but no appeal lies from a denial based on lack of a labor certification.

The approval of a *new* petition for the same beneficiary acts as a revalidation of the original petition.

Regulations Relating to Petitions in General

Petitions must be prepared in duplicate, every question therein truthfully answered, and signed with the full, true and correct name of the petitioner. They are executed under oath or affirmation in the United States, before an immigration officer (without fee) or notary public (the oath may also be taken before an officer authorized generally to administer oaths, in which case his official seal or certificate of authority must be affixed); outside the United States, the oath or affirmation must be made before a U.S. consular or immigration officer.

The importance of supplying correct information is emphasized by the fact that severe penalties are provided by federal law for knowingly and wilfully falsifying or concealing a material fact, or presenting any false supporting document.

A fee is charged for the filing of each petition, payable by check or money order to the "Immigration and Naturalization Service, Department of Justice" (except that remittances in Guam must be payable to "Treasurer, Guam;" and in the Virgin Islands, to "Commissioner of Finance, Virgin Islands").

Chapter 5
EXCLUDABLE ALIENS

No alien will be issued a visa if the consular officer knows or has reason to believe that he is ineligible to receive one; nor, whether or not in possession of appropriate documents, be permitted to enter the country if found on arrival at a port of entry to be excludable under the immigration laws. These laws clearly specify the grounds for exclusion in the case of both immigrants and nonimmigrants.

Any alien may reasonably assume, however, that he will not be denied entry if he can establish that he does not come within an excludable class, and provided further that he:

1. Applies in person at a place designated as a port of entry for aliens.

2. Applies at a time when the immigration office at the port is open for inspection of applicants for admission.

3. Makes his application in person to an immigration officer.

4. Presents whatever documents are required. An alien who obtains admission without complying with these requirements may be deported at any time.

The immigration laws also provide that whenever the President of the United States finds that the entry of any alien or class of aliens would be detrimental to the interests of the country, he may by proclamation, and for as long a period as he believes necessary, suspend the entry of all or any class of aliens as immigrants as nonimmigrants, or impose any restrictions on entry he considers suitable.

The reader should bear in mind that the grounds of *exclusion* and *deportation,* while frequently overlapping, apply to distinct areas. Deportation refers to the expulsion of aliens who have violated laws or regulations providing such a penalty AFTER being admitted to the country. Exclusion refers to denial of admission of aliens found excludable UPON SEEKING ENTRY.

It will be noted in the following exposition that some grounds for exclusion are mandatory; some discretionary; some applicable only to immigrants; and others to all aliens entering for either temporary or permanent stay. Excludable aliens are classified in this chapter according to certain categories to which the prescribed grounds for exclusion are specifically directed.

Persons Having Physical or Mental Defects

This class includes aliens found on medical examination to be:

1. Mentally retarded, insane (or to have had one or more attacks of insanity).

2. Narcotic addicts or chronic alcholics.

3. Afflicted with psychopathic personality, sexual deviation, or mental defect.

4. Afflicted with any dangerous contagious disease.

The physical and mental examination of all arriving aliens is conducted by medical officers of the U.S. Public Health Service, or contract-location or panel physician (employed on a temporary basis). Findings of the former are binding on a consular officer, but he may refer those of the latter to the Public Health Service for review.

An alien excludable because of tuberculosis, mental retardation, or history of mental illness, who is the parent, spouse, unmarried son, daughter, or minor adopted child of a citizen, resident alien, or alien issued an immigrant visa, may apply for waiver of excludability. The application is filed at the American Consulate at which the alien is applying for a visa, or, if in the United

States and applying for status as a permanent resident, with the immigration office having jurisdiction over the applicant's place of residence. There is no fee, but the application must be accompanied by specified supporting documents.

SUPPORTING DOCUMENTS: An alien afflicted with tuberculosis, applying for a waiver of excludability, must submit the following:

1. Statement by a state, territorial, or local health department, or recognized hospital or other institution for treatment of tuberculosis. Unless the U.S. Public Health Service has recognized the institution as satisfactory for such treatment, its statement must bear an endorsement by a health department affirming the latter's recognition of the institution. The statement must contain (a) name and address of institution where the alien will be treated; (b) affirmation that on arrival the alien will be placed in inpatient or outpatient status as determined by the responsible local physician; (c) affirmation that financial arrangements for care have been made by a sponsor or other responsible person, or that the applicant has established eligibility under the Department Medical Care Act of June 7, 1956; (d) agreement to supply any treatment and observation needed for proper management of the applicant's condition in accordance with accepted local standards of medical practice; (e) agreement to submit to the U.S. Quarantine Station, Rosebank, Staten Island, New York an initial report of clinical evaluation, including necessary x-ray films, within 30 days after applicant's arrival at the institution (or if he has not reported to the institution, a report to that effect within 30 days after notice from the U.S. Public Health Service that he has arrived in this country) and a report of final disposition of the case.

2. Assurance that on admission to this country he will go directly to the institution, submit to the required examination, treatment, and observation until discharged.

3. Assurance that, if applicable to his case, he will comply with the "Sanitary Measures for Travel of Aliens with Known or Suspected Tuberculosis" of which he will be given a copy.

An alien who is mentally retarded or has a history of mental illness, applying for a waiver of excludability, must submit a statement that he has arranged for filing a medical report, containing: (a) a complete medical history, including details of any hospitalization, institutional care or treatment for any physical or mental condition, findings as to his current physical condition, including chest x-rays if he is 11 years of age or over, serologic test for syphilis, if 15 years of age or over, and other pertinent diagnostic test; (b) findings concerning his current mental condition, information as to prognosis and life expectancy, and report of examination by a psychiatrist, and, in the case of mental retardation, also an evaluation by the psychiatrist of his intelligence; (c) in the case of a past history of mental illness information on which the U.S. Public Health Service can base a finding as to whether he has been free of such illness for a period sufficient to demonstrate recovery. (The report is referred to the U.S. Public Health Service for review, and if found acceptable, the applicant must submit any additional assurances which the Service deems necessary).

As noted earlier, an excludable alien, requiring immediate medical attention before inspection by an immigration officer may be admitted on parole for such purpose.

Persons Likely to Become Public Charges

This ground for exclusion relates to an alien who is:

1. Certified by a medical officer as having a physical defect, disease or disability determined by either a consular or immigration officer to be of such a nature as to affect his ability to earn a living, *unless* he proves tht he will not have to earn a living.

2. A pauper, professional beggar, or vagrant.

3. Likely at any time to become a public charge in the opinion of the consular or immigration authorities.

These provisions are designed to prevent the entry of aliens likely to require public assistance and includes not only the impoverished but also those who may be institutionalized for mental or moral deficiencies and those likely to be confined in jails or asylums.

There is no fixed rule as to the amount of money an alien should have, but it should be generally sufficient to provide for his reasonable wants and those of accompanying dependents until such time as he is likely to find employment, and to purchase transportation to his point of destination. Offers of financial assistance will not in themselves present an objection to admissibility.

Any alien excludable on this ground may, in the discretion of the immigration authorities, be admitted on giving bond assuring that he will not become a public charge.

Companions of Excludable Aliens

Any alien accompanying another alien certified by a medical officer as helpless because of illness, mental or physical disability, or infancy, and ordered excluded and deported, must also be excluded if his protection or guardianship is required by the other alien.

Persons Who Have Committed Crimes

This ground for exclusion relates to an alien who:

1. Has been convicted of a crime involving moral turpitude, other than a purely political offense.

2. Admits commission of such a crime or acts constituting the essential elements thereof under the laws of the country where the acts occurred. However, one who has committed only one such crime while under the age of 18 years may be granted a visa and admitted, provided the act occurred over five years before application for a visa or admission. If the crime resulted in confinement for any term, however, the alien must have been released more than five years before applying for a visa or admission. An alien excludable because of commission of a misdemeanor classifiable as a "petty offense" because of the punishment actually imposed, or an offense classifiable as a misdemeanor because of the punishment which might have been imposed, may be granted a visa and admitted if he committed or admits the commission of only one such offense. A "petty offense" is a misdemeanor punishable by not more than six months imprisonment, $500 fine, or both.

3. Has been convicted of two or more offenses, other than purely political, for which the aggregate sentences actually imposed were five years or more, regardless of whether (a) the offenses arose from a single scheme of conduct; or whether (c) the offenses involved moral turpitude.

4. A narcotic law violator or illicit trafficker in narcotic drugs. This refers to a person who has been convicted of a violation, or conspiracy to violate any law or regulation relative to the manufacture, possession, or traffic in narcotics or marihuana. It also includes anyone who the consular or immigration officer knows or has good

reason to believe is or has been an illicit trafficker in such drugs. The term "narcotic drugs" covers a number of synthetic or chemically compounded opiates as well as natural herbs and plants defined as addiction-forming or addiction-sustaining opiates.

Whether a crime involves "moral turpitude" depends upon the moral standards generally prevailing in the United States. A "purely political offense" is one where it is clearly established that the conviction was obviously based on "trumped-up" charges or repressive measures against racial, religious, or political minorities. However, the mere fact that the alien is or was a member of such a class will not in itself warrant any conclusion that he was convicted of a "purely political offense." Any alien excludable because of a crime involving moral turpitude, conviction of two or more offenses involving five or more years imprisonment, or involvement in prostitution, who is the parent, spouse, or child (including a minor unmarried adopted child) of a U.S. citizen or resident alien, may apply for waiver of excludability on Form 1-601. This will be granted, and the alien admitted, if the Attorney General is satisfied that exclusion would work extreme hardship on the relative citizen or resident alien, and that admission will not be contrary to the national welfare, safety, or security. The decision, however, lies in the Attorney General's discretion, and if favorable, may be on such terms and conditions as he considers necessary to impose.

Immoral Persons

This general category includes aliens who are:
1. Polygamists (other than nonimmigrants) who engage in or advocate the practice (not those who merely belong to a religious order which tolerates it).

2. Prostitutes, or former prostitutes, or anyone coming to engage in this profession, either primarily or incidentally. "Engage in" contemplates activity having elements of continuity and regularity, indicating a pattern of behavior or deliberate course of conduct, as distinguished from casual or isolated acts.

3. Persons coming for the *primary* purpose of engaging in immoral sexual acts.

4. Procurers, or persons who directly or indirectly have procured, or attempted to procure or import prostitutes or persons for purposes of prostitution or other immoral purposes (whether or not the latter be aliens).

5. Persons who have received, directly or indirectly, in whole or in part, the proceeds of prostitution.

6. Persons coming to engage in any other unlawful, commercialized vice, whether or not related to prostitution.

Surplus Workers

This ground of exclusion applies to aliens not having a certification by the Secretary of Labor (of the non-availability of like labor in the United States and in the locality of intended employment, and that such employment will not adversely affect wages and working conditions of those similarly employed in this country), who are any of the following:

1. Nonpreference immigrants.

2. Members of the professions or persons with exceptional ability in the sciences or arts (3rd Preference Immigrants).

3. Skilled and unskilled workers (6th Preference Immigrants).

4. "Special immigrants" (in the sub-category of natives of Western Hemisphere or Canal Zone countries—other

than parents, spouses, or children of U.S. citizens or resident aliens). (Such certification, however, is not required of elderly or other applicants who can prove that they will not seek employment).

Persons Offending the Immigration Laws

This category includes aliens who:

1. Have previously been involved in immigration proceedings, including those:

A. Excluded and deported: they may not be issued a visa within one year following deportation unless permission to apply therefor has been obtained from the Immigration and Naturalization Service.

B. Arrested and deported: these require permission to reapply, regardless of the time lapse since deportation.

2. Have been removed at their own request because of financial distress.

3. Have been removed as enemy aliens.

4. Have departed at government expense, in lieu of deportation. Such aliens must first obtain permission to apply or reapply for visas. Application is made on Form 1-212, together with a fee, mailed to the immigration office where removal proceedings were held, and showing the grounds relied on (e.g., that the alien's absence is causing unusual hardship to persons lawfully in this country; or that he is a bona fide crewman with no other means of livelihood; or that it is necessary for him to cross the border to buy necessities in connection with his business, or for some other urgent reason).

5. Seek admission from foreign contiguous territories or adjacent islands on non-signatory or non-conforming transportation lines (except in the cases of: natives of such territories or islands; aliens who have resided there for at least two years after arrival; resident aliens (of the

United States); "special immigrants" who are natives of the Western Hemisphere or Canal Zone; nonimmigrants; aliens who were not ineligible for visas at the time of their last previous entry; and aliens who first went to Canada on signatory lines, and thence to this country).

6. Were previously admitted as bona fide representatives of a foreign information medium, or as specialists to participate in a program designated by the Secretary of State, and seek visas without having resided in the country of their nationality or last residence or in some other foreign country for at least two years following departure from the United States. However, this requirement is deemed satisfied if the Secretary of State finds that the period of residence has served the purpose of the Mutual Education and Cultural Exchange Act of 1961, or it may be waived upon the favorable recommendation of the Secretary of State, or the request of an interested U.S. Governmental Agency or the Commissioner of Immigration and Naturalization, upon determining that departure of the alien from the United States would impose exceptional hardship on his spouse or child (if the latter be a citizen or resident alien), and if admission of the alien is found by the Attorney General to be in the public interest.

7. Have practiced fraud or wilful misrepresentation in procuring entry documents or seeking actual entry; or knowingly, and for gain, aided or abetted another alien to seek entry or enter in violation of law. This exclusionary ground does not apply to bona fide refugees who, for fear of repatriation, misrepresented their birthplaces in applying for entry to a country other than the United States, if these facts are admitted on applying for a visa to this country, and such mispresentation was not for the purpose of evading U.S. quota restrictions or investigation of their records at their former places of residence or

elsewhere, in connection with visa applications. (Fraud in actual entry may disqualify for later entry, but does not disqualify for application for a visa (this requires fraud in procuring entry documents)). Aliens excludable for fraud or misrepresentation in procuring visas or in entering (or who admit perjury in connection therewith) who are spouses, parents, or children of U.S. citizens or resident aliens, may be granted visas and admitted in the discretion of the Attorney General. Application for such waiver is made on Form 1-601, accompanied by a fee.

8. Are not in possession of proper entry documents, unless these have been or are waived (as explained in Chapter 3 and 4).

9. Are stowaways.

Illiterates

This denotes aliens unable to read and understand any language, except:

1. Resident aliens returning from temporary visits abroad.

2. Aliens not over 16 years of age.

3. Aliens physically incapable of reading.

4. Aliens coming to avoid religious persecution.

5. Parents, spouses, sons and daughters of citizens or resident aliens (accompanying or following to join them) (a son or daughter of a U.S. citizen, or an accompanying alien eligible for a visa, may confer his or her exemption as to literacy on a parent or grandparent).

6. Nonimmigrants.

The literacy test consists of showing the prospective immigrant a slip of paper or cardboard on which is printed in plain, legible type 30 to 40 words ordinarily used in the various foreign languages or dialects. The alien may select the language or dialect in which he wishes to be examined.

Aliens Ineligible for U.S. Citizenship

This denotes aliens (other than nonimmigrants) who, on or after September 8, 1939, departed or remained out of this country to evade military service.

Security Risks

This class includes aliens who are known or believed by consular or immigration authorities to be:

1. Seeking entry to this country, to engage in activities prejudicial to the public interest, or endangering the welfare, safety or security thereof, whether such purpose be primary and exclusive, or incidental in connection with other activities or purposes.

2. Likely, after entry, to engage in any activity:

A. Subversive to the national interest; or prohibited by laws relating to espionage, sabotage, or public disorder.

B. Whose purpose is opposition to, or overthrow and control, of the U.S. Government by force, violence, or other unlawful means.

3. Likely, after entry, to join, become affiliated with, or participate in the activities of, any communistic organization required to be registered with the Attorney General. Under the Subversive Activities Control Act (effective September 23, 1950) a communist organization must register as a *communist-action* or *communist-front* group. A "communist-action" group is part of the world-wide communist organization, controlled and directed by, and subject to the discipline of a foreign communist dictatorship, seeking to carry out the objectives of the communist conspiracy, which includes violent overthrow of the U.S. Government and establishment of a communist dictatorship. It includes the Communist Party of any State or foreign country and any other organization which promotes the cause of communism, or any section,

branch, affiliate, or subdivision thereof (as well as its predecessor or successor), e.g., youth or school societies; women's auxiliaries; factory or industrial chapters. In carrying on their activities, such groups are often organized on secret conspiratorial bases, operating through other organizations, known as "communist-fronts," created and used in such a way as to conceal their actual character, purpose, and membership. Such organizations are often able to obtain financial and other assistance which would not be forthcoming if the contributors knew the true purposes and actual source of control of such organizations.

It should be noted that no immigrant or nonimmigrant belonging to this category is exempt from exclusion with the exception of top level foreign government officials, by reason of Presidential sanction, and certain international organization officials.

Subversives

This class covers aliens who at any time were:

1. Persons opposed to government or law. This includes the teaching or advocacy of:

A. Opposition to all organized government.

B. Overthrow of the Government of the United States or all forms of law by force, violence, or other unconstitutional means.

C. The duty, necessity, or propriety of unlawfully assaulting or killing officers of this or any other form of government because of their official character.

D. Unlawful damage, injury, or destruction of property.

E. Sabotage.

F. Anarchy.

2. Persons who write or publish, or cause to be written or published, any matter advocating or encouraging the

ideas or conduct just described; or who knowingly take part in the circulation, distribution, printing, or display of such matter, or have it in their possession for any such purpose.

3. Persons advocating a totalitarian form of government, i.e.,

A. Support the establishment of a totalitarian dictatorship in the United States. A totalitarian dictatorship is defined as a system of government not in fact representative of the people, in which the policies of a single political party and those of the government are so similar that they cannot be distinguished, and in which any opposition to such party is forcibly suppressed.

B. Favor any of the economic, governmental, or international doctrines of world communism or support the establishment of a totalitarian or communistic dictatorship in the United States.

C. Write, publish, or knowingly print, circulate, distribute, or display any written or printed matter advocating the doctrines of world communism or establishment of a totalitarian dictatorship in the United States (or cause any of these things to be done; or knowingly have any such matter in their possession for any such purpose).

4. Persons who at any time have been voluntary members of organizations or parties advocating the ideas or purposes just described. This includes any who:

A. Join or affiliate with any group of persons favoring world communism, or creation of a dictatorship in the United States.

B. Belong to any communistic organization or party in the United States, in any State, or in any foreign country, irrespective of the name by which it has been known, now uses, or may adopt in the future (this refers to the Communist Party of the United States, the

Communist Political Association, Communist or any other totalitarian party in any country, including any section, branch, subsidiary, subdivision, or affiliate of any such organization or party).

C. Belong to, or are affiliated with, any organization which writes, prints, circulates, distributes, displays, or publishes any written or printed matter advocating any of the aforementioned ideas or conduct (or causes any of these things to be done; or possesses such written or printed matter for any of said purposes).

D. Join or affiliate with any organization at a time when the latter is, or is required to be, registered as a *communist-action* or communist-front group under the laws of the United States.

(Voluntary membership in a noncommunist party or organization (including any section, subsidiary, or affiliate) which, although totalitarian in nature, does not or did not advocate a totalitarian dictatorship in the United States, does not render a prospective immigrant ineligible for a visa. Existing regulations has removed members of Nazi and similar parties and organizations from the excludable class under this interpretation. However, if consular inquiry discloses that an individual member personally advocates, or has advocated, a totalitarian dictatorship in this country, he may be barred).

INVOLUNTARY MEMBERSHIP IN PARTY OR ORGANIZATION: Excludability for membership in or affiliation with a proscribed party or organization does not extend to aliens who can establish that their *past* membership or association was involuntary, i.e., that it:

1. Terminated before attainment of the age of 16.

2. Was caused by operation of law, i.e., came into being automatically, and without the alien's approval, by official act, order, edict, proclamation, or decree.

3. Was for the purpose of obtaining employment, food rations, or other necessities of life, and was necessary for such purpose.

The term "affiliation" is broader than the term "membership." It includes the giving, lending, or promising of money, services, or anything of value in support of the doctrine or organization espoused. The contribution of money or services includes the making of any gift, subscription, loan, advance, or deposit of money or anything of value, or the rendering of any service, as well as any promise or agreement to contribute or serve. Moreover, anyone who advises, recommends, professes or admits belief in, or assists by an overt act, the purposes, practices, procedures, aims or policies of a subversive organization is considered an affiliate of such organization and an advocate of its purposes. Helping to print or distribute any matter advocating subversive ideas or conduct brings an alien within this definition, whether such publication be a circular, newspaper, periodical, pamphlet, postcard, or leaflet.

Voluntary service in the armed forces of any country does not in and by itself constitute affiliation with a proscribed party or organization, unless it be in a political capacity, such as that of a political commisar serving with the armed forces.

VOLUNTARY MEMBERSHIP AND REDEMPTION: Excludability based on voluntary membership or affiliation will not attach to an immigrant who proves to the satisfaction of both consular and immigration officers that:

1. He has terminated such membership or affiliation, and, for at least five years before applying for a visa, has actively opposed the ideology, doctrine, principles and program of such party, organization, subdivision, or affiliate; and

2. His admission would be in the public interest.

GENERAL EXCEPTIONS: Nonimmigrant foreign government officials (thier families and employees) and foreign government representatives to international organizations (attendants, servants, personal employees, and members of their immediate families) are not affected by the just discussed exclusionary ground. However, the derivative exemptions (i.e., families and employees) are granted only on the basis of reciprocity.

Exclusion Hearings

If an applicant does not appear to be clearly and beyond a doubt someone who is entitled to land in the United States, he may be held for a hearing in front of a U.S. immigration judge.

An exclusion hearing to determine an applicant's right to enter the United States is held before the right to enter is granted.

In contrast, a deportation hearing to determine an applicant's right to be or remain in the United States is held after the applicant has already entered the country.

Rights of Detained Applicants.

The applicant for admission can only be detained in order that a hearing to determine whether or not he will be allowed to enter may be held.

The proceedings take place before a U.S. immigration judge and are not public unless the applicant asks for a public hearing. The applicant can be represented by a friend or an attorney. The decision of the judge must be based solely on the evidence produced at the hearing.

The decision made must be supported by evidence that would rationally prove that the person is not entitled to land in the United States. The evidence must have "rational probative force."

The judge may give his decision, orally or in writing. If the decision is given orally, the applicant must immediately make it known that he intends to appeal if that is the case. If the decision is given in writing, the applicant has 10 days from the date on which it is given to launch his or her appeal.

It is up to the judge's discretion to allow the applicant to post a bail bond or to be released on parole with or without a bond.

If the judge enters an *Order for Exclusion,* and the applicant does not appeal, he has no choice about where he will be deported. The applicant must be returned immediately to the country from which he came. But applicants in such cases may now apply for political asylum at exclusion hearings.

After the Decision
Sometimes applicants are returned to their native countries immediately on the same ship or plane that brought them to the United States. The carrier must bear the expense of transportation. Only the Attorney General may defer the deportation of an excludable person.

Admitting people from foreign countries to the United States is viewed as a privilege granted by the United States government, and it is granted only on the terms established by the United States.

The applicant for admission has the responsibility of proving that he is someone who clearly and beyond a reasonable doubt entitled to land in the United States.

Therefore, the constitutional guarantees and privileges do not apply to exclusion hearings. The courts have decided that there are basic differences between the exclusion proceedings where the applicant stands at the door and deportation proceeding where the applicant is already in the United States.

Deportation Hearing

As noted earlier, at a deportation hearing a person's right to be or remain in the United States is at stake. A deportation is a civil, not a criminal, proceeding so that some constitutional prohibitions do not apply. *Ex post facto* laws are therefore applicable to the person about to be deported.

Rights of Applicant

If the applicant is charged and detained by the Immigration Service he is entitled to "due process" in the conduct of the hearings. This means that the applicant (1) is entitled to receive notice of the charges made against him, (2) is to have the opportunity to examine the evidence against him and to cross examine witnesses testifying against him, and (3) to have the right to present evidence on his own behalf.

Furthermore, the applicant has all the constitutional rights and privileges, including the Fifth Amendment right against self-incrimination, that a citizen has.

At the deportation proceeding, the Immigration Service is responsible for showing by "clear, unequivocal, and convincing evidence" that the applicant is an alien who is deportable.

The decision made by the immigration judge must be passed solely on the evidence presented at the hearing (*e.g.,* no secret reports or rumors are to be considered).

The judge who presides over the deportation hearing must make certain decisions. He must determine whether or not the applicant is a person who is deportable under the Nationality Act (which sets out more than 700 grounds for deportation).

It must also be determined whether or not the applicant will be allowed to make a voluntary departure, or whether he should be granted an adjustment of status to permanent resident. The applicant may be granted or denied the privilege of a "creation of a record of lawful admission" if, for example, he entered the United States illegally or without proper documentation before June 30, 1948.

The judge also has power to withhold and suspend the deportation or terminate the deportation proceedings altogether.

The applicant may be arrested and detained in custody and can be released from custody pending a hearing if he posts a bond or files a personal recognizance. Whether or not this can be done is in the discretion of the District Director. However, the applicant would not likely be detained unless it was found that he was a poor bail risk or a threat to national security.

At the hearing, the Immigration Service argument will be presented by an attorney who is designated by the District Director. This person can be a lawyer or an immigration officer.

The applicant can represent himself, or can be represented by a friend or an attorney. If the applicant cannot afford to hire an attorney, the Immigration Service is obligated to inform the applicant that he may be entitled to the services of a legal aid attorney. Applicants now have the right to be represented by an attorney at the hearing as long as it is without cost to the government.

Many deportation hearings involve students who have violated their status by failing to obtain an extension of stay, failing to obtain permission to transfer to another school, or by working without permission.

Relief Available

After all the evidence has been heard, the judge may make an order indicating that one or more of the following steps are to be taken.

(a) The alien shall be deported.
(b) The proceedings against the alien are to be terminated.
(c) Deportation shall be suspended.
(d) Applicant alien will be granted the right to depart voluntarily in lieu of deportation.
(e) Other action, within the discretion of the judge, can be taken in order to dispose of the proceedings.

At a deportation hearing the judge must ask the applicant where he wants to be deported. If the judge does not ask, the applicant may have grounds for an appeal to the Board of Immigration Appeals.

In addition to the rights discussed thus far, the applicant can make applications for discretionary relief at deportation hearings. He may apply for a stay of deportation on Form I-256 through a District Director or make a motion to reopen or reconsider An Order of Deportation. The applicant may file a Request for Asylum in the United States to ask that he not be deported to a country where he may be persecuted because of his race, religion or political opinions.

The applicant may also have his status adjusted from nonimmigrant to permanent resident. He should make this application on Form I-485, the Application for Status as Permanent Resident.

In addition, the applicant must establish that he is eligible to be granted this status and will have to show that he had been inspected or paroled for admission into the United States on an immigrant visa in one of the categories available to him or her.

The applicant must have maintained his visitor or temporary worker status by not continuing or pursuing unauthorized employment after January 1, 1977 unless he had permission from the Immigration Service or is an immediate relative of a U.S. citizen.

The applicant may not apply for an adjustment of status to permanent resident if he is a crew member, an exchange visitor who has not had the two year foreign residence requirement waived, a person who entered while in transit to another country, or if the applicant entered the country without inspection or entered fraudulently.

Suspension of Deportation

The applicant can ask for a suspension of deportation on Form I-256 if he can show that he was continuously and physically present in the United States for the previous 7 years or performed honorable service in the armed forces of the United States for at least 24 months.

The applicant must also show that he has been of good moral character and that deportation would cause extreme hardship to the applicant, a spouse, or minor children if they are United States citizens or lawful permanent residents of the United States.

If the applicant has been convicted of criminal, immoral, or subversive acts and is a person who is deportable then he must show that he was physically a resident in the United States for at least 10 years. The applicant must also show that his family would suffer extreme and unusual hardships if the applicant was deported.

All suspension cases are reported to the Congress on the first day of each month when Congress is in session. In the case of seven year suspension cases, if Congress takes no action before the close of the session following the one in which the case is reported, suspension of deportation becomes final.

In cases based on ten year physical presence and good moral character in the United States, if suspension is not approved by Congress, the application for suspension of deportation shall not be approved by the Immigration Service.

In order to file an Application for Suspension of Deportation, the applicant must provide numerous supporting documents and have them ready to present to the judge at the hearing.

Some of these will be affidavits of good character and gainful employment.

Copies of all the documents are to be brought to the deportation hearing so that the applicant can keep the originals. All documents should be translated if not already in English. If the applicant has one, he should submit any temporary entry permit that he was given upon entry into the United States.

It is important to remember that in order to obtain the suspension the applicant must show that deportation would result in extreme hardship to a United States citizen or permanent resident to whom the applicant is closely related by blood or marriage.

Documents such as a birth or marriage certificate are used to establish a relationship to the people who would suffer if the applicant was deported.

A divorce decree or death certificate may also be needed to establish the validity of a marriage or the existence of a close relationship to a United States citizen or lawful permanent resident.

A naturalization certificate may also be needed, but under no circumstances should it be photocopied. The applicant could be fined for doing so.

In order to establish that the applicant has continuously resided in the United States for seven years the applicant can produce items such as bankbooks, leases, deeds, licenses, letters, church records, school records, employment records, and tax receipts.

The applicant must also show the judge that during his stay in the United States he was a person of good moral character. In order to do this, the applicant will show police records from all areas where he lived during the past seven or more years.

Two United States citizens have to sign affidavits in which they say, under oath, that they knew the applicant for a specified period of time, and during that time they formed a good opinion of his character.

An affidavit from an employer stating that the applicant's general reputation as to character was good during the period of employment must also be produced.

With the Application for Suspension the applicant must also file two photographs of himself or herself and pay a filing fee.

Deported At Own Expense
The applicant may ask that he be allowed to leave the United States at his own expense and thereby avoid having an Order of Deportation filed against him. In order to bring this application, the applicant must have been a person of good moral character for at least five years prior to the hearing and must show that he is willing and has enough money to leave the United States promptly.

If the applicant is granted this relief, he can apply to have the date of voluntary departure extended. If this relief is denied, he is still considered to be deported according to law. Therefore, before applicant can reenter the United States, he must obtain the permission of the Attorney General on Form I-212. It is a criminal felony and a violation of the immigration laws to return to the United States after deportation without permission from the Attorney General. At any time during the deportation hearings, the applicant is entitled to make a motion to reopen or reconsider the proceedings. In order to do this, the applicant must file a written motion which either sets out new evidence that was not previously available, or states why the applicant claims that an erroneous interpretation of the law or abuse of discretion was made.

Rights of Appeal To The Board of Immigration Appeals

The applicant can appeal a decision by a United States immigration judge in a deportation or exclusion proceeding to the Board of Immigration Appeals in Washington, D.C. unless he is a crew member, a stowaway, or a person excluded on security grounds or for medical disqualifications.

Applicant must always be notified of his right to appeal when a decision is made against him. As noted earlier, if the decision is given orally, applicant must immediately notify the judge of his intention to appeal. If the decision is made in writing, applicant must file a written appeal within 10 days. Usually, when an applicant is notified of his right to appeal, instructions will be given on how to carry it out.

The reasons on which the applicant bases his appeal must relate to questions of law, procedural questions, standards of evidence, or the arbitrary exercise of discretion by the immigration judge.

Judicial Review of Deportation Order

A deportation order, or the denial of the various kinds of relief available at a deportation hearing, may be reviewed by filing a Petition for Review with the United States Court of Appeals after all administrative remedies within the INS have been tried.

The petition to Review a Deportation Order must be filed within six months after a final ruling by the Board of Immigration Appeals. It is filed in the registry for the United States Court of Appeals of the circuit in which the applicant resides or in which the deportation hearing was conducted.

The applicant may not obtain a judicial review if he has been served with a final Order of Deportation and has departed from the United States. The Court of Appeals will look solely at the record of the appealed proceedings. No new evidence will be admitted.

Judicial Review of Exclusion Order

After the applicant has appealed to the Board of Immigration Appeals from an exclusion proceeding, he has only the right to petition the district court for a review of the administrative action taken in the exclusion hearing. The appeal will ask the district court to inquire into whether or not the exclusion hearing was a fair hearing and whether or not the Order of Exclusion was supported by substantial evidence and based on grounds provided in the Immigration Act. The proper name for this petition is a Petition for Writ of Habeas Corpus. In order to make use of it, the applicant must first have gone through the Board of Immigration Appeals and not have left the country after the exclusion order was issued.

There are some 700 grounds for deportation. Sections 212 adn 241 (a) and (c) of the Immigration and Nationality Act contain some of them.

Chapter 6

UNITED STATES CITIZENSHIP THROUGH NATURALIZATION

United States citizenship is acquired in one of two ways: by birth or by *naturalization*. Anyone born in the United States and subject to its jurisdiction, even though the parents are not citizens, is a U.S. citizen by birth. Also, children who were born abroad to parents who are American citizens are citizens of the United States.

STATUTORY PROVISIONS: Any person who has been admitted to the United States as an immigrant for permanent residence may apply for naturalization to become an American citizen using Form N-400 Application to File Petition for Naturalization.

An applicant for naturalization must have been lawfully admitted to the United States for permanent residence and have lived continuously in the United States for at least five years, or three years if the alien is a spouse of an American citizen.

The applicant should have held an Alien Registration Form I-551 for at least five years if he is married to a U.S. citizen. He must be a person of good moral character (i.e., must not have been arrested for five years). He must be able to read, write and speak the English language and have a knowledge of the history and government of the United States. He will be required to understand and answer five or six questions picked at random and put to him by the naturalization examiner. He may be required to write in English the following sentence: "The first President of the United States was George Washington." He will have to say that he believes in or values the principles of the United States Constitution.

People who have been legal permanent residents in the United States for 20 years and who are at least 50 years old qualify for U.S. citizenship without having to demonstrate proficiency in English.

OATH OF ALLEGIANCE TO UNITED STATES: The final hearing to become an American citizen takes place in a United States district court or an authorized state court where the formal ceremony is completed and the Oath of Allegiance to the United States is taken. He will receive notice of the naturalization ceremony which should take place within 60 days of the hearing. At the close of the ceremony a Certificate of Naturalization is given to the applicant.

WHO QUALIFIES FOR CERTIFICATE OF AMERICAN CITIZENSHIP: If the applicant was born before May 24, 1934, in order to be able to apply for a Certificate of Citizenship one has to show that the father was a citizen before he was born. The citizenship of the mother is not considered.

If the applicant was born on or after May 24, 1934 and before January 13, 1941 to parents who were both citizens, one parent had to reside in the United States before he or she was born. If only one parent was an American citizen, then that parent must have lived in the United States for some period of time before the birth of the applicant.

In addition, the applicant must have lived in the United States for a minimum of 5 years between the ages of 13 and 21 before he can apply. If the American parent was employed by an American organization abroad, the applicant may retain his citizenship if he took up American residence in the United States before applicant was 16 years old and before December 24, 1952.

If the applicant cannot meet these requirements, he can retain citizenship by showing that he was physically present in the United States for at least 2 years when he was between 14 and 18 years old. The 2 years' physical presence applies to anyone born on or after May 24, 1934.

If the applicant was born on or after January 13, 1941, and before December 24, 1952 and both parents were American citizens, there are no problems. If only one parent was an American citizen, that parent must have lived in the United States or its possessions for at least 10 years, and at least 5 of those years must have been after reaching 16 years of age. If the American parent served honorably in the armed forces between December 7, 1941 and December 24, 1952, then 5 years of the 10 year U.S. residence period may be calculated after the parent reached 12 years of age.

The applicant child of the marriage must in this case have lived in the United States or any of its outlying possessions between the ages of 13 and 21 for a period of not less than 5 years. If the applicant lived in the United States before reaching the age of 16 and he shows that he was physically present in the United States before reaching 16 years of age but after the December 24, 1952 deadline it must be shown that a 2 year continuous physical presence in the United States between the ages 14 and 28 took place.

If the applicant was the legitimate child born to American citizen parents after December 24, 1952, then he need not comply with any residency requirements. If, however, only one of the parents was an American citizen, that parent must have lived in the United States for 10 years, and 5 of those years must have passed after the parent turned 14. If the applicant child of the marriage was born between December 24, 1952 and October 10, 1978, he must show that he lived in the United States for at least 2 years when applicant was between the ages of 14 and 28. Children born after October 10, 1978 can retain U.S. citizenship without living in the United States.

The new law is not retroactive, however, and anyone

who had lost U.S. citizenship under the former law would not have it restored to him or her presently.

ILLEGITIMATE CHILDREN: In this situation the applicant's right for a Certificate of Citizenship depends on the status of the mother and on whether or not the father legitimated the birth.

If the applicant was born before May 24, 1934, he acquired American citizenship at birth if the mother was a citizen who lived in the United States before the applicant's birth. If the father was an American citizen who legitimated the applicant's birth to someone who was not a citizen (i.e., married applicant's mother or adopted him legally) then the applicant acquired citizenship as of the date of birth as long as the father was an American citizen who had previously lived in the United States or outlying possessions.

If the applicant was born on or after May 24, 1934, then he acquired citizenship on the date of birth as long as the mother was an American citizen who had lived in the United States before the applicant was born. If the father was an American citizen who later legitimated the applicant's birth, he acquired citizenship as of the date of his birth as long as he had resided in the United States or outlying possessions before birth. If applicant was born on or after January 13, 1941 and before December 24, 1952, then he acquired citizenship at birth as long as the mother was a citizen who had lived in the United States before applicant's birth. If applicant's paternity was established when he was underage, then the father must have been a citizen when he was born, and the father must have had 10 years residence in the United States and 5 of those years must have been spent in the United States after turning 16.

If applicant was born on or after December 14, 1952, he acquired citizenship from the American mother as long as she had lived in the United States for one year continuously before applicant's birth.

If applicant was legitimated while under 21 years of age and both parents were citizens and at least one parent had lived in the United States prior to applicant's birth, he acquired citizenship as of birth.

If applicant was legitimated while under 21 and only one parent was an American citizen, the citizen parent must have been physically present in the United States or one of its outlying possessions for at least 10 years, 5 of which passed after he turned 14 and before applicant was born. He must have resided continuously in the United States for at least 5 years when between the ages of 14 and 28.

WOMEN WHO LOST THEIR CITIZENSHIP ON MARRIAGE: For women who lost their U.S. citizenship by marrying an alien, there are several provisions for regaining citizenship.

Women who marry aliens today may resume citizenship simply by taking the Oath of Allegiance. Since December 24, 1952, a woman who lost citizenship by marriage to an alien after September 22, 1922 has been able to resume citizenship by taking the oath.

For marriages prior to the 1922 date, the woman resumed citizenship on July 2, 1940 if she had lived in the United States continuously from the date of marriage until July 2, 1940. In order to exercise the rights of citizenship, she has to take the Oath of Allegiance.

For marriages that were terminated, the resumption of citizenship depends on when the marriage terminated and where the woman was living.

If applicant lived in the United States at the time the marriage was terminated, some special factors must apply so that citizenship can be gained promptly. If applicant lived outside of the United States, there are certain residence or registration requirements.

If the marriage was terminated on or after March 2, 1907 and before September 22, 1932, and applicant lived in the United States at the time, then she does not have to do anything. Her citizenship was resumed immediately on termination. If she lived somewhere other than the United States, then she would have had to return to the United States before September 22, 1922 or registered with the American consul for the country of your residence within one year of the termination of her marriage.

If the marriage was terminated on or after September 22, 1922 and before June 6, 1936, then citizenship was resumed on July 2, 1940 if the woman had resided in the United States continuously from the date of marriage. This provision applies to native-born women and includes those women who were born abroad and who acquired citizenship at birth and lost their citizenship because they married an alien before September 22, 1922.

If she was residing outside of the United States when her marriage was terminated, the applicant's citizenship was resumed on July 25, 1936, if not previously resumed. All women whose marriages terminated in this time period have to take the Oath of Allegiance before they exercise the rights of an American citizen.

Those whose marriages terminated before January 13, 1941 and after July 25, 1936 had their citizenship restored immediately whether they lived abroad or in the United States. In either case, they must take the Oath of Allegiance before exercising the rights of citizenship.

If the marriage to an alien was terminated on or after January 13, 1941, the woman can resume her citizenship by taking the Oath of Allegiance before a clerk of the naturalization court. If she lived abroad, she can take the Oath of Allegiance before an American consular office.

In all cases where the marriage was terminated after September 22, 1922, the applicant must have been a native born citizen or have acquired citizenship at birth if born abroad. Furthermore, the applicant must take the Oath of Allegiance before exercising the rights of a citizen.

CHILDREN BORN TO LAWFUL PERMANENT RESIDENTS: If one of applicant's parents was naturalized before May 24, 1934, he can claim U.S. citizenship if the naturalization took place before his 21st birthday. He must have been registered as a lawful permanent resident before May 24, 1934 and before his or her 21st birthday. His citizenship begins five years after acquiring lawful permanent resident status.

If one of the parents was naturalized on or after May 24, 1934 and before January 13, 1941 than the applicant child can claim citizenship if the naturalization took place before his 21st birthday, and if he was lawfully admitted to the United States as a permanent resident before his 21st birthday.

In addition, the child must have lived for five years as a lawful permanent resident in the United States. The five years must have begun before the child's 21st birthday and before January 13, 1941. Note that in the case of people whose parents were naturalized before May 24, 1934, but who were not admitted to the United States until after the date, all of the above requirements applicable to the residence of the child apply.

The five year residence requirement of the child can be waived if both parents are naturalized, or if the surviving parent or divorced parent with legal custody is naturalized.

If the parents were naturalized on or after January 13, 1941 and before December 24, 1952, then the following circumstances must be present: Both parents (one, if child had only one parent as a result of death or divorce) must have become naturalized. If one parent was an alien and the other a citizen, then the alien must have become naturalized within that period. In addition, the parent or parents must have become naturalized before the child's 18th birthday and the child must have been lawfully admitted as a permanent resident before his 18th birthday.

If the applicant is a child born to an unmarried woman during this period, then the child cannot claim American citizenship unless legitimated by an American citizen before he turned 16 in accordance with the law of his or her residence at that time.

If the parents were naturalized on or after December 24, 1952, then both of them or the noncitizen parent must have become naturalized within this period. If the child has only one parent as a result of death or divorce, he must have become naturalized within that period. The parents' naturalization must have taken place before the child's 18th birthday and the child must have been admitted as a lawful permanent resident before his 18th birthday. The residence requirements for a child also apply if the child was born out of wedlock, legitimated before he was 16 years old, and in the custody of the legitimating parent. The child must also meet these residence requirements if no paternity was established yet the parent remained a resident of the United States.

Children who were born outside the United States and who are under the age of 16 when adopted by U.S. citizens may now apply for permanent residence immediately after entering the United States. In the past, a two-year residence period was required.

Readers, who think that they might qualify to recover lost citizenship or acquire it by birth, should check with their nearest INS or American consulate. They will assist you in determining whether or not you should apply for a Citizenship Certificate.

LOSS OF CITIZENSHIP: A citizen may lose citizenship through *denaturalization or expatriation. Denaturalization* is the judicial revocation of the naturalization order based on a finding that the naturalization was illegally or fraudulently obtained. Of course, *denaturalization* applies only to naturalized citizens. But *expatriation* applies to both natural-born and naturalized citizens and does not assume a defect in the original acquisition of citizenship. *Expatriation* results from certain actions enumerated in the law by which the citizen voluntarily relinquished his or her citizenship.

Grounds for Denaturalization

(1) Naturalization may be revoked if the certificate of naturalization was "procured by concealment of a material fact or by willful misrepresentation" or was "illegally procured."

Facts suppressed or concealed in a naturalization proceeding are "material" if disclosure of those facts alone would justify denial of citizenship. But the test of materiality also includes concealed facts which, if disclosed, would have led to the investigation and discovery of other facts bearing on the applicant's eligibility for naturalization.

There must be intentional concealment to constitute concealment or misrepresentation within the meaning of the law. Specific concealments and misrepresentations which courts have found sufficient to warrant *denaturalization* include: deliberate suppression of criminal records where there is a duty to disclose; knowingly false statements concerning marital or family status; and deliberate misstatement concerning an applicant's fulfillment of the residence requirements.

(2) Illegal procurement is an independent ground to revoke naturalization. The term has been held to convey

something wider in scope than fraud, not restricted to intentional deception. It has included naturalizations procured when prescribed requirements—for example, attachment to the principles of the Constitution or lack of good moral character—had no existence in fact. The term also encompasses affirmative misconduct by the applicant to induce the court or governmental agents to act in a manner not authorized by law. It also includes the granting of certificates upon error of law, for example, as to jurisdiction or procedural irregularities such as denying the government the opportunity to question the applicant in open court or to introduce evidence.

However, the error must be substantial to justify denaturalization. Clerical mistakes in connection with the issuance of a naturalization certificate will not constitute grounds for revocation and errors of judgment in granting citizenship against the preponderance of the evidence are better corrected on appeal in the original naturalization proceeding than in an action to revoke naturalization.

(3) The statute provides that if a naturalized citizen takes up permanent residence in a foreign country within five years after naturalization, it shall be considered *prima facie* evidence of lack of intention to establish permanent residence in the United States at the time of the petition for citizenship. In the absence of countervailing evidence, this *prima facie* evidence is sufficient to justify revocation of naturalization, as having been obtained by concealment of a material fact or by willful misrepresentation.

The naturalized person may rebut the presumption by testimony that he intended in good faith to establish permanent residence in the United States. The courts tend to grant the defendant every reasonable doubt and show great receptiveness to consideration of extenuating circumstances.

(4) The denaturalization statute provides two additional grounds for revoking naturalization: (a) Refusal on the part of the naturalized citizen, within ten years following his naturalization, to testify before a congressional committee concerning his subversive activities, will be grounds for revocation of naturalization, if such refusal resulted in a conviction for contempt. The refusal to testify establishes as a matter of law that naturalization was procured by concealment of a material fact or by willful misrepresentation and the naturalized citizen is not granted an opportunity within this provision to present countervailing evidence. (b) If within five years of naturalization a naturalized citizen becomes a member of any of the prescribed subversive organizations, of which membership would have precluded naturalization in the first place, it shall constitute *prima facie* evidence that such person was not attached to the principles of the Constitution at the time of naturalization. In the absence of countervailing evidence it will be sufficient to revoke the person's citizenship as having been obtained by concealment of a material fact or by willful misrepresentation. However, neither ground has been invoked in any naturalization proceeding to date and the constitutionality of these provisions may be in doubt because of the discrimination they impose on naturalized citizens.

Expatriation:

Expatriation is the second means for loss of nationality, to which both naturalized and native born citizens are subject. The term is defined as the *voluntary* act of abandoning one's country and becoming the citizen or subject of another. Under present Supreme Court rulings, the specific intent of the alleged expatriate to renounce citizenship must accompany the expatriating act, in order to constitute relinquishment of citizenship.

There are several methods of expatriation:

(1) *Obtaining naturalization in a foreign state.* Subject to the constitutional requirement of voluntariness, statutes provide that a person who is a citizen may lose his nationality by obtaining naturalization in a foreign state, either upon personal application, or that of a parent or duly authorized agent, or through the foreign naturalization of a parent having legal custody of such person. But an accompanying proviso states that a person shall not lose citizenship because of his parent's foreign naturalization; unless such person fails to enter the United States and establish permanent residence prior to his twenty-fifth birthday. It appears, however, that obtaining naturalization in a foreign state is only evidence, although persuasive, of intention to relinquish United States citizenship.

(2) *Oath of allegiance to a foreign state.* If a citizen takes an oath or other formal declaration of allegiance to a foreign state, he is expatriated under the present law. The courts will inquire if the person taking the oath actually intended to abandon United States citizenship. If the oath is taken in circumstances indicating lack of voluntariness, such as military conscription, the requisite intent to transfer allegiance may not be found.

(3) *Military service in a foreign state.* If a citizen without the prior written authorization of the Secretary of State and the Secretary of Defense enters the military service in a foreign nation, he may be expatriated. An exception for persons entering foreign military service before their eighteenth birthday provides that such service will cause expatriation only if there exists an option to secure release, which the citizen fails to exercise upon attaining age eighteen.

(4) *Foreign government employment.* Employment in the government of a foreign state coupled with (as a condition of employment) acquisition of nationality in or

declaration of allegiance to the foreign state will serve as grounds for expatriation. This broad language has, however, been restricted by the courts. For example, in a California court case, the petitioner had taught public school in Japan during and after World War II for which the United States government claimed she was expatriated. A federal district court disagreed, focusing not only on the voluntariness question but upon the nature of the government service. Teaching school, the court reasoned, was not the type of foreign government employment envisioned by the Act, which was intended to encompass service to a foreign government the performance of which required absolute allegiance to the foreign government. Teaching did not come within this category.

(5) *Formal renunciation of nationality.* Making a formal renunciation of nationality before a diplomatic or consular officer of the United States in a foreign country will lead to expatriation if performed in a manner prescribed by the Secretary of State. Informal renunciations of citizenship are ineffective, however, as are other methods not meeting the State Department methods.

If renunciation occurs in the United States it must be in writing and during time of war to take effect. The Attorney General is empowered to designate the officer to receive such renunciations and to promulgate procedures for accepting them. The current statute has not been invoked, although a prior version was used to expatriate several citizens of Japanese descent during World War II.

(6) *Acts of treason and subversion.* A citizen shall lose nationality if convicted of committing any act of treason against the United States or of conspiring to incite insurrection against the government.

Chapter 7

PERSONS WHO CLAIM BUT ARE DENIED RIGHTS AS NATIONALS OF THE UNITED STATES

Any person outside of the United States who claims but is denied a right or privilege as an American national by an agency, official, or department of the Government (such as being refused a passport, or denied a petition to grant "immediate relative" or "special immigrant" status to a spouse or child) on the ground that he is not an American national, may apply to a consular or diplomatic officer of the United States in the country where he is residing for a "Certificate of Identity" for use in travelling to a port of entry in this country, where he will then apply for admission. Such a certificate is available, however, only to persons who at some time prior to making application, have been physically present in this country or persons under 16 years of age born abroad to a United States citizen parent.

If the application is denied, the applicant may appeal to the Secretary of State. There is some conflict in the lower courts as to whether an action will lie to compel issuance of such a certificate by the Secretary of State. It has been held both that it will not, and that it will if denial by the Secretary of State is arbitrary.

If the application is granted and the certificate issued, the recipient may apply for admission at any port of entry, where a determination of his claimed citizenship status will be made by immigration authorities. If their decision is adverse, the applicant may appeal to the Board of Immigration Appeals and to the Attorney General of the United States. A final administrative determination that he is not entitled to admission as a citizen may be reviewed only by a petition to a federal district court in habeas corpus proceedings.

Procedure for Obtaining Certificate of Identity

Application for a "Certificate of Identity" is made in quadruplicate on Form FS-343 (revised), signed and sworn to in person before a diplomatic or consular officer. It must contain statements showing:

1. That the applicant claims to be a national of the United States.

2. The basis for such claim and the reason for claiming a right or privilege as a U.S. national.

3. That the application is made in good faith and upon a substantial basis.

4. That the right or privilege claimed has been denied by a specified department, agency, or official of the United States on the ground that the applicant is not a national (indicating the date and place of such denial).

5. That the applicant has instituted an action against the head of such agency or department in the U.S. District Court for the District of Columbia or for the district where he claims permanent residence.

6. That the applicant desires to proceed to the United States to prosecute such action and understands that, if losing and failing to depart as then directed, he will be subject to deportation.

The application must also be accompanied by an affidavit of a credible witness sworn to before such officer (unless the latter waives the requirement of submitting such affidavit). In addition, it must be accompanied by four photographs, taken within 30 days of filing the application (two inches square; unmounted; on thin paper, against a light background, and showing a clear, front view of the applicant's features, without headdress, unless he is a member of a religious order which wears the same). The distance from the top of the head to the point of the chin must be approximately one and one-fourth inches. Snapshots, group, and full length pictures are unacceptable. The applicant must sign (or, if incapable, make a mark) on each copy of the photograph, with his full and true name, in such a manner as not to obscure the features. One copy is glued to the original application, and one to each copy thereof, impressed with a legend machine so as not to cover the features. Offices having no legend machine may use the impression seal (which must always be used in completing the application). Also, the applicant's fingerprints must be attached to the original application and each copy.

In considering an application for a Certificate of Identity, the diplomatic or consular officer, insofar as practicable, also makes an independent investigation into the facts.

Chapter 8

ILLEGAL IMMIGRATION AND REFUGEES

Illegal aliens are aliens who have violated the immigration law, hence the designation "illegal." Most enter the United States surreptitiously, bypassing inspection. A small number enter the United States legally, generally as nonimmigrants, and violate the terms of their admission, usually by overstaying and accepting unauthorized employment.

The phrase "illegal alien" is a popular expression, rather than a term defined in the Immigration and Nationality Act. It replaced the more colloquial term "wetback" which was widely used throughout the fifties. In the past several years, the term "illegal alien" has increasingly been replaced by "undocumented alien," out of sensitivity to the concerns of the Mexican government and others who find the designation "illegal alien" objectionable because of the connotation of criminality. Other synonymous terms are illegal immigrant, undocumented worker, and deportable alien.

The number of illegal or undocumented aliens in the United States is not known. INS currently estimates the illegal population as ranging from 3 to 5 million. The problem is generally agreed to be primarily an economic one, both in its causes and its effects. The primary, though not the only, effects of illegal immigration are believed to occur in the labor market. There is increasing disagreement about the nature and extent of these effects in such areas as the displacement of United States workers, and the impact on wages and working conditions. There is also disagreement as to whether the effects are primarily negative. With regard to causes, the major impetus behind the illegal migration to this country is generally seen to be the economic imbalance between the United States and the countries from which the aliens come. They come here primarily to obtain employment and to escape poverty for themselves and their families.

In addition to concern about the economic implications, increasing attention is focused on the foreign policy implications of the problem, particularly as it relates to Mexico. However, while illegal or undocumented aliens are widely believed to be predominantly Mexican, evidence shows that they are by no means solely from Mexico. Chairman Peter Rodino of the U.S. House Judiciary Committee, and formerly of the sub-committee with jurisdiction over immigration, noted as far back as 1972:

> "When we first commenced these hearings it seemed that the problem was focused on the Mexicans and the illegal alien was the Mexican.
>
> It was the judgment of this Member, as the chairman of this committee, that as we went on it wasn't just the Mexican; that illegal aliens come from every area. We must remember that the visitor who overstays is also an illegal alien."

Probably the least controversial aspect of the illegal or undocumented alien issue is that it represents such a widespread violation of the immigration law that the viability of the law is called into question. In the words of one House Judiciary Committee report, "This wholesale violation of the law disrupts the legal and orderly flow of aliens into the United States, and threatens the integrity of our system of immigration."

The provisions of the Immigration and Nationality Act relating specifically to illegal or undocumented aliens are summarized here. Under section 275 (8 U.S.C. 1325), any alien who enters the United States without examination by INS or through misrepresentation or fraud, is guilty of a misdemeanor punishable by up to 6 months' imprisonment and a $500 fine or both. A second offense is a felony, punishable by not more than 2 years' imprisonment and/or a $1,000 fine. Section 276 (8 U.S.C. 1326) provides that an alien who was previously deported and who enters without permission from the Attorney General is guilty of a felony punishable by not more than 2 years' imprisonment, and/or a fine of $1,000.

Section 274 of the Immigration and Nationality Act (8 U.S.C. 1324) defines the smuggling, harboring, transporting, or encouraging of illegal entrants as felonies, punishable by a fine not exceeding $2,000 and by imprisonment for a term not exceeding 5 years, or both for each alien involved; it also provides for the seizure and forfeiture of vehicles used in illegal transportation. However, the law specifically exempts the employment of illegal entrants from the penalties attached to harboring. Section 274(a)(4) contains the following proviso: "*Provided, however,* that for the purposes of this section, employment (including the usual and normal practices incident to employment) shall not be deemed to constitute harboring."

Aliens who accept employment or otherwise violate the conditions of their admission are subject to deportation under section 241(a)(9) of the Act (8 U.S.C. 1251)(a)(9), which provides that an alien shall be deported if he "was admitted as a nonimmigrant and failed to maintain the nonimmigrant status in which he was admitted or to which it was changed pursuant to section 248, or to comply with the conditions of any such status." Aliens who accept unauthorized employment are also prohibited to from adjusting their status from that of nonimmigrant to that of permanent resident alien (immigrant) while remaining in this country (sec. 245(c); 8 U.S.C. 1255c).

Again, as noted earlier in this chapter, the proposed Simpson-Mazzoli legislation pending in Congress at the time of this publication must be referred to by the reader once its passed in final form.

DIRECTORY OF INS OFFICES

Following are the addresses of the INS District Offices and Suboffices where papers may be filed. When more than one district is located in a state, you will need to check with one of the offices to determine and correct jurisdiction for filing your papers. Correspondence should be addressed to "Immigration and Naturalization Service, U.S. Department of Justice." Note: Addresses and telephone numbers may change.

I. Northern Region
Federal Building
Fort Snelling
Twin Cities, MN 55111
(612) 725-4451
 A. Anchorage District
New Federal Building
701 C St.
Room D229
Anchorage, AK 99513
(907) 271-5029
  1. Fairbanks Suboffice
P.O. Box 60208
Fairbanks, AK 99706
(907) 452-3307
(Accepts papers for fil-
ing only)
 B. Chicago District
Dirksen Federal Office
Building
219 S. Dearborn St.
Chicago, IL 60604
(312) 353-7334
  1. Indiana Suboffice
46 E. Ohio St.
Room 148
Indianapolis, IN 46204
(317) 269-6009
  2. Wisconsin Suboffice
Federal Building
Room 186
517 E. Wisconsin Ave.
Milwaukee, WI 53202
(414) 291-3565

 C. Cleveland District
Anthony J. Celebrezze
Federal Building
Room 1917
1240 E. 9th St.
Cleveland, OH 44199
(216) 522-4770
  1. Cincinnati Suboffice
J.W. Peck Federal
Bldg.
550 Main St.
Room 8525
Cincinnati, OH 45202
(513) 684-3781
 D. Denver District
1787 Federal Office
Building
1961 Stout St.
Denver, CO 80202
(303) 844-3526
  1. Utah Suboffice
230 W. 400 South St.
Salt Lake City, UT
84101
(801) 524-5690
 E. Detroit District
Federal Building
333 Mt. Elliot St.
Detroit, MI 48207
(313) 226-3290
 F. Helena District
Federal Building
Room 512
301 South Park

Drawer 10036
Helena, MT 59626
(406) 449-5288
  1. Idaho Suboffice
    4620 Overland Road
    Boise, ID 83705
    (208) 334-1821
G. Kansas City District
  Suite 1100
  324 E. 11th St.
  Kansas City, MO 64106
  (816) 374-3421
  1. St. Louis Suboffice
    210 N. Tucker Blvd.
    Room 100
    St. Louis, MO 63101
    (314) 425-4532
H. Omaho District
  Federal Office Building
  106 S. 15th St.
  Room 1008
  Omaha, NE 68102
  (402) 221-4651
I. Portland District
  Federal Office Building
  511 N.W. Broadway
  Portland, OR 97209
  (503) 221-2271
J. St. Paul District
  927 New Post Office
    Building
  180 E. Kellog Blvd.
  St. Paul, MN 55101
  (612) 725-7107
K. Seattle District
  815 Airport Way, South
  Seattle, WA 98134
  (206) 442-5959
  1. Spokane Suboffice
    691 U.S. Courthouse
      Building
    W. 920 Riverside
    Spokane, WA 99201
    (509) 456-3824

II. Eastern Region
Federal Building
Elmwood Avenue
Burlington, VT 05401
(802) 951-6254
A. Baltimore District
  E.A. Garmatz Federal
    Building
  101 W. Lombard St.
  Baltimore, MD 21201
  (301) 962-2120
B. Boston District
  John F. Kennedy Federal
    Building
  Room 700
  Government Center
  Boston, MA 02203
  (617) 223-0201
  1. Connecticut Suboffice
    3060 Ribicoff Federal
      Building
    450 Main St.
    Hartford, CT 06103
    (203) 249-4222
  2. Rhode Island Suboffice
    Federal Building
    Room 203
    U.S. P.O. Exchange
      Terrace
    Providence, RI 02903
    (401) 528-5315
C. Buffalo District
  68 Court St.
  Buffalo, NY 14202
  (716) 846-4731
  1. Albany Suboffice
    Post Office Building
    Room 227
    445 Broadway
    Albany, NY 12207
    (518) 472-2434
D. Newark District
  Federal Building
  970 Broad St.
  Newark, NJ 07102

E. New York District
26 Federal Plaza
New York, NY 10278
(212) 206-6500
F. Philadelphia District
Room 1321
U.S. Courthouse
Independence Mall West
601 Market St.
Philadelphia, PA 19106
(215) 597-7333
 1. Pittsburgh Suboffice
 2130 Federal Building
 1000 Liberty Ave.
 Pittsburgh, PA 15222
 (412) 644-3356
G. Portland District
76 Pearl St.
Portland, ME 04112
(207) 780-3352
 1. Vermont Suboffice
 Federal Building
 P.O. Box 328
 St. Albans, VT 05478
 (802) 524-6742
H. San Juan District
Federal Building
Room 170
Charlton St.
Hato Rey, PR 00936
(809) 753-4280
 1. St. Croix Suboffice
 P.O. Box 1270
 King Shill
 Christian Sted,
  St. Croix, VI 00856
 (809) 772-3500
 2. St. Thomas Suboffice
 Federal Building
 P.O. Box 610
 Charlotte Amake, St.
  Thomas, VI
 (809) 774-1390
I. Washington D.C. District
25 E. St., N.W.
WA, D.C. 20538
(202) 724-7796

 1. Virginia Suboffice
 Norfolk Federal
  Building
 200 Granby Mall
 Room 439
 Norfolk, VA 23510
 (804) 441-3081)

III. Southern Region
First International Building
1201 Elm St.
Room 2300
Dallas, TX 75270
(214) 767-6024
 A. Atlanta District
 Room 1408
 Richard B. Russell Federal
  Building
 75 Spring St., S.W.
 Atlanta, GA 30303
 (404) 221-5158
  1. North Carolina
   Suboffice
  1111 Hawthorne Lane
  Building C
  Charlotte, NC 28205
  (704) 371-6691
  2. South Carolina
   Suboffice
  Federal Building
  Room 110
  334 Meeting St.
  Charleston, SC 29403
  (850) 724-4350
 B. Dallas District
 Room 6 A21
 Federal Building
 1100 Commerce St.
 Dallas, TX 75242
 (214) 767-0514
  1. Oklahoma Suboffice
  Federal and
   Courthouse Bldgs.
  200 N.W. 4th St.
  Room 4415
  Oklahoma City, OK
   73102
  (405) 231-4121

C. El Paso District
   343 U.S. Courthouse
   P.O. Box 9398
   El Paso, TX 79984
   (195) 541-7625
   1. New Mexico Suboffice
      517 Gold Southwest
      Ave.
      Room 1114
      Albuquerque, NM
      87103
      (505) 766-2378
D. Harlingen District
   2102 Teege Ave.
   Harlingen, TX 78550
   (512) 425-7333
E. Houston District
   2627 Caroline
   Houston, TX 77004
F. Miami District
   7880 Biscayne Rd.
   Miami, FL 333138
   (305) 350-5741
   1. Jacksonville Suboffice
      Post Office Building
      Room 227
      311 Monroe Street
      P.O. Box 4608
      Jacksonville, FL 32201
      (904) 791-2624
   2. Tampa Suboffice
      Federal Building
      Room 539
      500 Zack St.
      Tampa, FL 33602
      (813) 228-2131
G. New Orleans District
   Postal Service Building
   Room T-8005
   701 Loyola Ave.
   New Orleans, LA 70113
   (504) 589-6533
   1. Kentucky Suboffice
      Room 601
      U.S. Courthouse
      Building
      W. 6th & Broadway

Louisville, KY 40202
      (502) 582-6375
   2. Tennessee Suboffice
      814 Federal Building
      Room 830
      167 N. Main St.
      Memphis, TN 38103
      (901) 521-3301
H. San Antonio District
   U.S. Federal Building
   Suite A301
   727 E. Durango
   San Antonio, TX 78206
   (512) 229-6350

IV. Western Region
    Terminal Island
    San Pedro, CA 90731
    (213) 548-2385
    A. Honolulu District
       595 Ala Moana Blvd.
       P.O. Box 461
       Honolulu, Hawaii 96809
       (808) 546-8920
       1. Guam Suboffice
          801 Pacific News
          Building
          233 O'Hara St.
          P.O. Box DX
          Agana, Guam 96910
          (671) 472-6411
    B. Los Angeles District
       300 N. Los Angeles St.
       Room 1000
       Los Angeles, CA 90012
       (213) 894-2119
    C. Phoenix District
       Federal Building
       230 N. First Ave.
       Phoenix, AZ 85025
       (602) 261-3122
       1. Tucson Suboffice
          Federal Building
          300 W. Congress
          Room 8-M
          Tucson, AZ 85701
          (602) 629-6228

2. Las Vegas Suboffice
Federal Building
Room 104
U.S. Courthouse
300 Las Vegas Blvd.
   South
Las Vegas, NV 89101
(702) 385-6251
3. Reno Suboffice
Suite 150
350 Center St.
Reno, NV 89501
(702) 784-5427
D. San Diego District
880 Front St.
Room 1-513
San Diego, CA 92188
(619) 233-7036
E. San Francisco District
Appraisers Building
630 Sansome St.
San Francisco, CA 94111
(415) 495-6667
1. Fresno Suboffice
U.S. Courthouse,
   Federal Building
1130 "O" St.
Room 1308
(209) 487-5091
2. Sacramento Suboffice
650 Capitol Mall
Sacramento, CA 95814
(916) 551-2785
3. San Jose Suboffice
280 S. First St.
San Jose, CA 95113
(408) 292-6624

V. Overseas Offices
A. Bangkok District
c/o U.S. Embassy
APO San Francisco, CA
96346

1. Hong Kong Suboffice
c/o American
   Consulate General
Box 30
FPO San Francisco,
   CA 06659
2. Manila Suboffice
c/o American Embassy
1201 Roxas Blvd.
APO San Francisco,
   CA 96528
3. Seoul Suboffice
c/o American Embassy
APO San Francisco,
   CA 06301
4. Singapore Suboffice
c/o American Embassy
FPO San Francisco,
   CA 06699
B. Mexico City District
c/o U.S. Embassy
P.O. Box 3087
Laredo, TX 78041
1. Guadalajara Suboffice
c/o American
   Consulate General
P.O. Box 3088
Laredo, TX 78044
2. Monterrey Suboffice
c/o American
   Consulate General
P.O. Box 3098
Laredo, TX 78044
3. Panama City Suboffice
c/o U.S. Embassy
APO Miami, FL 34002
C. Rome District
c/o U.S. Embassy
APO New York, NY 09794
1. Athens Suboffice
c/o U.S. Embassy
APO New York, NY
   09253

2. Frankfurt Suboffice
   c/o American
      Consulate General
   Box 12
   APO, New York, NY
      09213

3. Naples Suboffice
   c/o American
      Consulate General
   Box 18
   FPO New York, NY
      09521

The following states have no INS office. These states come under the jurisdiction of the district listed with the state. You must check with that district to see whether the state is serviced by a suboffice within the district.

Alabama (Atlanta)
Arkansas (New Orleans)
Delaware (Philadelphia)
Iowa (Omaha)
Kansas (Kansas City)
Mississippi (New Orleans)

New Hampshire (Boston)
North Dakota (St. Paul)
South Dakota (St. Paul)
West Virginia (Philadelphia)
Wyoming (Denver)